THE SACRED HUB

Living In Our Real Self

ROBERT RABBIN

New Leaders Press
in association with
Hamsa Institute

The Sacred Hub
Living In Our Real Self

Copyright © 1995 by Robert Rabbin
Published by New Leaders Press, San Francisco, California
in association with Hamsa Institute.
Printed in the United States of America.

Hamsa Institute
20 Sunnyside Avenue, Suite 118–A
Mill Valley, CA 94941

Publisher's Cataloging in Publication
Rabbin, Robert
    The sacred hub: living in our real self / Robert Rabbin.
    p. cm.
    ISBN 0-9630390-8-3
    Library of Congress Catalog Card Number: 95-69828

1. Self (Philosophy) 2. Spiritual life. 3. Meditation. I. Title
BD450.R33 1995   126
                                        QBI95-20256

The cover is an original oil painting depicting the Hindu god Shiva, the Lord of the Universe, whose ecstatic transcendent dance creates the whole cosmos. Shiva is that pure consciousness which pervades the entire universe. This image of Shiva shows him emerging from the blue field of supreme consciousness to destroy the illusions of the mind and thus reveal the sacred hub of the universe within each person's heart.

Cover art and design by Claudia Gioseffi, Blue Sky Studio
Book design by Sergio Mello, SVM - designs
Back cover photo by Rosalie Wardell, Wardell Media

ACKNOWLEDGEMENTS

This book is dedicated with profound gratitude to Swami Muktananda Paramahamsa, the embodiment of grace.

I am happily indebted and grateful to the following people, all of whom have been tremendous friends and staunch advocates of the Hamsa Institute:

Monika Pichler, who has been my best friend, counsel, and frequent collaborator for the past ten years. She is truly an embodiment of love, and her light has on innumerable occasions revealed what I could not see;

Eddie Oliver, Rick Rabbin, and Sandra Rabbin for their steadfast love, encouragement, and support over the years;

Janine Sagert, John Renesch, and Dorothy Divack for their contributions to this book; and

All those friends, clients, and participants in Hamsa seminars with whom I have been able to roam in the space of the sacred hub. They have been the living inspiration for this material.

I am grateful beyond words to Dan Whalen and Bonnie & Mike Shingleton for their faith in this project. Their kind hearts and financial generosity funded the publication of this book.

INVOCATION

WHERE THERE IS SUFFERING AND PAIN,
MAY THERE BE HEALING AND EASE.

WHERE THERE IS ANGER AND OPPRESSION,
MAY THERE BE FORGIVENESS AND FREEDOM.

WHERE THERE IS HATRED AND VIOLENCE,
MAY THERE BE PEACE AND COMPASSION.

WHERE THERE IS POVERTY AND SORROW,
MAY THERE BE ABUNDANCE AND JOY.

WHERE THERE IS IGNORANCE,
MAY THERE BE WISDOM.

WHERE THERE IS FEAR,
MAY THERE BE LOVE.

AUTHOR'S NOTE

These writings were spontaneous compositions, written without deliberation. They were written in the crucible of silence and only after the heat and current of that silence appeared. Many times I would feel a gentle hand squeeze my heart, my eyes would fill with tears, and, suddenly, my fingers would move across the keyboard. Whenever I attempted to edit the "ideas" during or after this way of writing, the process stopped and I could not continue.

That didn't stop me from trying to edit. I wanted the material to be something other than what it was. I wanted what was written to be graspable; I wanted definitive explanations and certain solutions. I wanted a more singular and consistent style. But there was always a voice that said, "Do not write to please the mind. Let what is beyond the mind speak to disrupt the mind." Some things are known only through being.

As I wrote at my pine desk, I felt surrounded by a presence which I call love. Looking out the window I would marvel at how beautiful the eucalyptus trees were, or how stunning the hummingbirds that hovered at the feeder were. Sometimes I would take a break and wander through the house or walk out to the garden, where I would sit silently. Sitting in this silence, I noticed that everything was translucent. A soft light emanated from everywhere. The trees towering above me, the distant hills and the bay beyond, the passing clouds, the clumps of dirt all seemed alive and breathing and radiant. Something I have no words for was at work where the eyes could not see. Though it cannot truly be spoken, it is real.

These writings are simply expressions from the place of silence that meditation and inquiry take me to. The content is not that important, because whatever can be said is not the truth. If there is value here, it is because you may be provoked to venture beneath the layers of the mind's false imaginings into the sacred hub within your own heart. There, you will find your own truth, your own expression, your own experience of the Self. Should this happen, then we are all served.

TABLE OF CONTENTS

THE SACRED HUB

Living In Our Real Self

PREFACE

In 1969, I lived in a wood shack near the village of Trinidad, about thirty miles north of Arcata, California. I was supposed to be studying Eastern philosophy at Humboldt State College but spent hardly any time in class. Instead, I sampled a variety of hallucinogens, sat zazen and practiced Aikido, followed the saga of Carlos Castaneda, and read haiku poetry — tiny bridges of words that are connected to the immense emptiness behind conventional thinking and meaning. During this time, I encountered the world of silence, and in that silence I first experienced that the physical world perceived by the senses was a mere tissue hiding something vast.

It was in search of that vastness that I traveled to India. In 1973, I set off with a friend whom I had met the year before in Israel. Eric and I had decided to go overland from Europe. We set off from Paris, hitchhiking to Brindisi, Italy, intending to take the ferry to Greece, and then trains and buses through Turkey, Iran, Afghanistan, Pakistan, and into India.

During one of the station stops in eastern Turkey, Eric and I ventured out to the platform, where we met another traveler, a Frenchman. Herve was a shepherd, returning to India to see his "guru," Swami Muktananda. The three of us struck up a friendship and journeyed together another two months, ending up in Delhi, India. We had endured and enjoyed much and had formed a great bond of love. In India, Herve invited us to visit him at his guru's ashram near Bombay. But Eric and I were headed to Bhutan, so as we parted company to go our separate ways, I was sure I would never see Herve again.

I never made it to Bhutan. I think that the vast silence I was searching for took control of my itinerary. I was first sent to a small ashram in the foothills of the Himalayas, where the resident guru, Neem Karoli Baba, had passed on just days before. I stayed there for about a week. During that time I heard many stories of Muktananda, and several people suggested I visit him.

Returning to Delhi, Eric decided that he wanted to study the sitar in Benares. I bought a third class ticket and boarded a train for Madras. My next adventure, courtesy of the silence, was a two week vipassanna meditation retreat with Goenka, a Burmese teacher. I subsequently visited Satya Sai Baba's ashram, and wandered around south India. Several months later, I ended up in Bombay. I thought of Herve.

I climbed into a battered red bus and spent the day crawling the 60 miles to see him in his ashram. I entered through the circular gate into the marble courtyard that is the entrance wearing sandals, white cotton pants and shirt, and carrying a small rucksack.

Herve was in a Bombay hospital, expected back soon, and Muktananda was up north in Kashmir with a few disciples. I was invited to stay as a guest until Herve's return. I settled into a tiny room with a cot and mattress and a view of the rice paddies and plantain trees. The ashram was quite beautiful and clean, a real oasis from the pounding I had taken wandering around India for five months. Herve returned two days later, and he became my enthusiastic guide through the ashram's rigorous discipline.

One was expected to wake up at 3:00 AM and pretty much remain engaged with meditation, chanting Sanskrit hymns, or work of one sort or another until 10:00 PM. As I was still but a guest, I was allowed some leniency. I managed a few hours a day of meditating and chanting, pitched in with the dishes and the gardening. Sometimes, a few of us would escape to the dingy yellowed tea shop next store, where in deep shadows we'd drink strong tea strained through a T-shirt unwashed in over a decade.

I began to get restless. I wanted to head up to Benares to meet Eric. Herve went nuts when I told him I wanted to leave. He insisted I wait a few more days to meet his guru. French shepherds can be very persuasive. I relented.

A few days later, a current of intense excitement went through the ashram. Muktananda was coming home. In the late morning, we all gathered densely in the front of the ashram with the usual cacophony signaling auspicious events: bells, trumpets, conches, gongs, and clapping, shouting, and stomping. Suddenly, there was the guru.

I spent several more seemingly uneventful days in the ashram. In Muktananda's presence, everyone seemed more alert and alive, almost on edge. I hadn't yet felt the hammer of recognition, which would come later in a series of excruciating inner experiences. Once again I felt it was time for me to head north and meet up with Eric, and I told Herve I really had to get moving. I think he felt sad for me that I hadn't connected with Muktananda in the way he had. Reconciled as he was to the mysterious ways of karma, he bowed to the inevitable. Or what we thought then was the inevitable. My wanderlust was inflamed. I was rested and ready for more adventures. Herve told me that it was customary good manners to request permission from Baba, which is what the devotees called Muktananda, to leave the ashram; after all, I had accepted his hospitality for over two weeks, and it was a gesture of respect. Not wanting to offend him or Baba, I agreed.

I had my small traveling bag packed and was within minutes of the next bus departure for Bombay. Baba was sitting on his small marble perch in the main courtyard, where he would often sit for hours, unperturbed by time or events. Even with my mind preoccupied with imminent departure, I was aware of a breathtaking aspect to Baba. To this day, I have not encountered anyone or anything as compelling as Baba just sitting on his cushions on that marble verandah. He was so fabulously dangerous. Anything could happen. Anything did happen.

I went up to him and said, "Baba, I've been in your ashram for a few weeks, but I have to leave now. Thank you very much for allowing me to stay here."

He looked at me for a moment and said, "Where are you going?" A reasonable and friendly question. I told him I wanted to go to Benares to meet a friend. He looked at me again, differently, as though he were an x-ray machine. Something in me quivered. "Why do you want to go to Benares?" he asked. "It's cold there at this time of year. It's cold in Benares."

At his last word I went totally blank. I can recall that something in me skipped a beat: it was a sudden disruption of complacency, like when you loose your balance and fall without warning. I was disoriented and confused, and I couldn't regain my inner balance. Then, I plunged into timelessness for an encounter with silence. I don't know how to describe those moments. I know it will sound odd, but I wasn't there: I disappeared. That's why I don't know what to say.

At some point in the aftermath of Baba's comment, I reappeared and steadied a bit, but I knew something wasn't quite the same. Some strange transfusion of energy had taken place. Soon, I was all right, or so I thought. I walked back to Herve, and blurted out, "I guess I won't be going to Benares." Herve cracked up.

There were many perfectly polite and rational things I could have said to Baba when he told me how cold it was in Benares, like "Yes, but I have warm clothes," or "Don't worry, I won't be there long." But something transpired in that exchange that to this day, 22 years later, I still can't quite fathom. My life took a radical turn. That moment foretold a dream I would have months later, in which Baba, holding my hand as we soared through space, whispered, "If you stay with me, I'll take you flying to places you've never been before."

Baba's guru, Bhagawan Nityananda, was reported to have said, "The heart is the sacred hub of the universe. Go there and roam in that space." I believe that the experience I still can't fathom pointed me irrevocably toward that sacred hub. I remained enthralled by Muktananda and remained under his tutelage for the next ten years.

I sometimes reflect on a conversation I had with Baba in his room in India, shortly before he passed away. He told me to return to America. He said I was to be his emissary. He said he would tell me where to go and what to do. At that time I thought he was referring to work he had asked me to do as an executive in his organization. Perhaps he did, perhaps he didn't. If there is one thing that is certain, it's that sages are quite inscrutable. Their words and actions have layers of significance, and some of the more subtle layers unfold over time. I don't think it is possible to understand a sage definitively. I don't think anyone can know with certainty or authority what a sage means when he speaks to a particular person, including the person to whom the sage speaks. I do think that behind everything a sage says is the basic commandment, "The heart is the sacred hub of the universe. Go there and roam in that space."

Looking back, I think that's what Baba meant. I think he meant that I should continue to roam in the sacred hub of the universe. He was showing me my path in this life. To be his emissary is to stand for the light of our own true nature, our essence, the Self. I think he meant that I should serve that Self and listen to that Self and follow that Self. Rumi, a Sufi poet of the Self, said the same thing in this way, "Keep the love of holy laughing in you. Don't visit sad neighborhoods." I think this is what Baba meant.

A few days after that conversation, I said goodbye to him as he sat on his chair in the courtyard. I began to slowly walk away, resigned to return to America. He called me one last time. As I turned to him, I saw he had leaned forward in his chair. He held a tiny candy in his right hand. With an impish and mischievous smile that contained all the love I could ever want, he said, "You should never leave the ashram without something sweet." That was the last time I saw him.

Over the years, I have tried to follow his instructions. I agree with J. K. Krishnamurti, who said that truth is a pathless land. The pathless path is not always clear, rarely certain, frequently terrifying, always challenging. Roaming in the sacred hub of the universe is simple, but it's not easy. Still, I think we should try.

What Baba said to me is an important message for everyone. I think we all know, intuitively, that our real home is the sacred hub of our own heart. I sincerely hope that we will all try to experience the truth of that sacred hub. If we do, I'm certain this planet will become the paradise it was intended to be.

INTRODUCTION

This book does not contain information or ideas the mind can readily comprehend and use. My statements are not solid answers; they are provocations for deeper questioning, deeper contemplation of how we are to live. In this contemplation of ourselves, we seek to examine thought itself, to uproot and discard all our false imaginings, so that we can live with innocence and purity. As one explores essential questions, one exposes limiting beliefs, mistaken identities, attachments, fears and tension, all of which obscure the true nature of the questioner. The more one exposes, the more one illuminates the questioner. The light that illuminates the questioner is the silence of the sacred hub.

One way to enter the sacred hub is through inquiry. Inquiry is simply the starting place from which to go deeper into the unplumbed depths of inner awareness. Questions that pertain to life should not be answered immediately, they should not be assaulted with what is already known. Rather, these questions should provoke careful and deep reflection about the question and about the questioner. This spiraling inquiry leads us beneath the conditioned mind, to awareness itself. The Indian poet Kabir once wrote, "I reached the place inside me where the world is breathing." It is into this billowing awareness that inquiry takes us.

The mind, of course, wants to understand, to grasp some specific meaning. Inquiry, however, does not provide this. Inquiry sabotages the mind and its need for security and certainty. Inquiry confounds the mind's patterns to allow the awareness behind the mind to reveal itself.

Through inquiry, we seek to awaken a capacity of self-knowledge which is deeper than thought and prior to the impressions of acquired knowledge. What we already know is of the past, a mote against new and fresh insight. Insight in the present is not conditioned by the past. Insight in the present is being, and it is this being, free and unconditioned by acquired knowledge, that inquiry awakens and arouses. The intelligence of our being is an innate capacity. It is wisdom. In arousing our innate wisdom, we can clarify ourselves and our actions. We can illuminate the very causes of conflict, doubt, and fear within us. This path of inquiry is a direct and unmediated way to realize our essential nature. When we discover our essential nature, when we recognize who we are — through deep and persistent inquiry — in this depth of silence we become free. This freedom is love, and this love is the purpose and fulfillment of life.

I have found, as perhaps you have, that there is a tremendous "knowing" that leaps into the mind when it is silent, when it has given up trying to understand, when all of its false imaginings and projections have been exposed. Inquiry take us into this depth of silence, and then the silence reveals itself like a primordial breathing. This kind of knowing is transmitted to us as pure revelation, unformed by words and images. It is like a potent dye released in an ocean that instantly permeates every drop. When we open ourselves to this deep unconditioned knowing, we too are completely permeated.

Entering this inner silence unifies and makes whole what had seemed piecemeal and fragmented. In this wholeness, we experience a oneness of being in which the tension of feeling separate from life disappears, in which internal and external conflicts are resolved in an encompassing clarity. I call this silent intelligence, this wholeness, the Self. The Self is not a thing, like a brick, nor is it an abstraction, like patriotism. The Self is pure, primordial awareness: the supremely intelligent current of life that enlivens and animates everything in existence. It is a fountain of insight and clarity, a presence that is the fragrance of reality. The guidance of the Self is what we all turn to in times of need. The Self is the sacred hub of the universe, out of which everything else appears, and around which everything revolves.

We have all experienced intimations of the Self and we have all experienced its cleansing effect on the confusion, fear, and doubt of the mind. The Self is outside of time, outside of convention, outside of expectation, outside of self-concept. It is an illumination in which everything merges into an ineffable oneness. It is a rapture of self-transcendence. This is the place in which the whole world breathes, and it is the place that is aroused and awakened through persistent inquiry into our lives and into the nature of the mind and of the separate self with which we normally identify. It is a place known to us, though we may not remember; familiar, though we may not admit it; treasured, though we may discount it; utterly real, though we cannot prove it.

Can you imagine trying to explain love to someone who has not experienced it? This is the irony of the Self. We are all searching for the love of the Self, but we cannot explain this to ourselves or to others. So we look for the Self where it isn't, in objects and ideas, and remain unfulfilled.

The Self can never be known in the way we know how to repair cars. It can never be measured, can never be proven. It simply is, without qualification or condition. The Self is beyond any measure, any knowing, any experience. The Self is always present, always moving from the hub to its spokes.

Modern science tells us that within our very own cellular structure is the imprint of energy released when the universe was first created, that we have the dust of ancient stars in our hair. We say this, but we don't actually grasp it. If we could actually grasp it, we would see in a flash that we are part of that supreme creative force that is even now creating and dissolving immense galaxies and dimensions whose measures cannot be taken. We would put everything else to the side, and give ourselves fully and freely to this force, which pulsates in each human heart as the Self.

When we enter this creative force of the sacred hub, we are able to answer the questions of living through being. The only impediment is the outward turned mind, which creates, projects, and identifies with false imaginings. In this way, we look for truth where it isn't. Our only problem is that we are estranged from the Self.

There is a natural expansion of awareness that occurs in silence. This silence emerges in a deep and profound relaxation of thinking when one turns the attention within. This expansive awareness is inherent to everyone. In this awareness, we glimpse the Self. This silent awareness speaks without words, with sudden clarity that is known through being.

We might think that only special people are endowed with this knowledge of the Self. But this knowledge of the Self is within each of us. All we have to do is see what is there, within us. We tend to discount our own capacity to know the Self now, as we are. We tend to distrust the spontaneous knowing that comes to us from silence, from the Self, because it often contradicts and violates the conventions of our own thinking.

Still, there is something within us which can hear reverberations from the place where the world is breathing. The mind can't fathom those things which are only known through being. When we face the vast, eternal silence of the Self, the mind stops. When the mind stops, an eruption of pure awareness pours through the gaps between our thoughts. In that timeless moment, we become what we are: the Self. The Self shines when the mind falls into the silent awareness that we have all experienced.

My teacher, Swami Muktananda, said that the love of the inner Self, of the divine flame, is alive within each of us. All we have to do is turn our attention inward. He said, "If you understand your own Self, you will never have to learn how to love, because you will become the embodiment of love. You are the source of love. Give up all your worries and try to understand who you are."

This love is the real teacher, the real teaching, the real path. This love is what we seek, and it is who we are. This love is the language of the Self. We should give ourselves freely to the Self. We should enter the sacred hub of the heart and live in our real Self. Here, with tears of rapture streaming from our grateful eyes, we will be what we are, restored through love to wholeness, peace, and joy.

PRESCRIPTION FOR LIVING

It is important to find out exactly what we want. I know this can be difficult, especially when so many people tell us what we should want and how we should get it. Each has their own unique prescription. We can't be persuaded by this, we must see for ourselves what is missing in our life.

The prescription that we accept should cure the condition that we have. For this, a clear diagnosis is required. We must each diagnose the truth of what we want, and we must determine this honestly. What exactly do you long for?

I first experienced the nature of deep longing when I was eleven years old. I had broken my leg skiing, and I had to lay in bed for a month with a cast up to my hip. I began perusing a set of encyclopedias. I didn't read them all. I just turned each page, book by book, and read what interested me. My mind opened wide. There were so many amazing things: the intricate dances of insects, the forces of nature, the distant galaxies, the gods and goddesses of strange religions. I remember being overwhelmed. I felt there was something behind all of this, but I couldn't put my finger on it. I had a faint intuition that something was moving silently behind the universes described in the encyclopedias. A wordless wonderment appeared within me, and questions formed like gathering clouds. How did all of this come about? Where did I fit in?

These questions lived within me, and I listened for answers. There were none. No one else seemed concerned with the vast universe and the mystery from which it came. No one asked questions. Everyone just went about their business. This way of living without questioning disappointed me.

I internalized that disappointment and became sad. My own questions became quiet, and I tried to fit in with life as it was offered to me. I did the best I could in school. I participated in sports and student government. I worked after school in a butcher shop. I learned to play the drums. But I was always disappointed and sad. I didn't know how to articulate this then. I was just aware of a constant emptiness, an ache. My friends were designing their lives with ambitious plans and goals, but I felt like an unsettled ghost. I was not interested in pursuing anything. I couldn't give my heart to what others where giving their hearts to.

One day the vague questions I had been harboring became clear. I was nineteen years old, and in my third and final semester of college. I was sitting with my girlfriend and our philosophy professor in a concealed part of the campus garden, which I had helped to plant. We had taken some mescaline.

Suddenly, from a pulsating sky, I was drenched by a monsoon of colors: crimson and wheat, sienna and rust. I trembled. The vividness of this was tremendous. Something in me shattered in that hallucinatory moment. In that shattering was an awakening. I can only say that the awakening was the question "Who am I?" This was the crystallization of the wonderment that had been born years before.

My own seeking intensified. Now I had clearly defined the condition for which I wanted a prescription. The condition was ignorance of my own self. I had to find out. How could one live without knowing this?

I sought out one adventure after another, hoping that in extreme conditions of living I might find an answer. I took up meditation and Aikido. I studied Eastern philosophies. I traveled restlessly to Europe and to Israel. I lived in mountains and deserts. I studied poetry and took up rock climbing. I lived in hashish dens. I traveled the arduous overland route to India. I remember reading Autobiography of a Yogi, by Yogananda, on a train in Turkey. It helped me realize there were others who had asked this question and who had something to say about it.

I wandered around India for several months. I met yogis, teachers, and gurus. I stayed in ashrams and sat in meditation retreats. I heard lectures and read scriptures. Still, my longing was un-fulfilled.

One day, in the fall of 1973, I walked into the ashram of Swami Muktananda, a meditation master. He was on a pilgrimage in Kashmir when I arrived, but I stayed on, nonetheless. Within a few days of his return, I had heard his basic prescription, one which he repeated constantly. Here is my summary of what I heard:

Everything is consciousness, and you are that conscious-ness. That consciousness is God, and you are that. You are beyond the body, beyond the mind, you are the one Self that shines everywhere. You are love. You are perfect. You are that consciousness which pervades the entire universe. Turn within and meditate on your own Self. When you know your own Self, you will know everything, because that Self is the creative, intelligent power behind this whole universe. To know your own Self is to know everything. Your inner Self is consciousness, and that consciousness is love, and that love pervades everything, everywhere. Dive deep within yourself and you will know this directly. Continue to meditate on your own Self, and everything else will happen at the right time.

Those words entered deeply, and I was very affected. A whole new world opened up within me. In the presence of Muktananda, I experienced the answer I had been looking for.

I continue to follow his advice. I continue to meditate on that inner Self. As I do so, there is a deepening awareness of the power of which he spoke at work in all things big and small, near and far. I have not found it necessary to follow other prescriptions.

If you want to know who you are, not as an idea or belief, but deeply, truly, directly, and you want that more than anything else, then this may work for you. At any rate, it is the only prescription I have ever taken, because it was the only one that entered deeply and had an effect on my condition. His prescription is the only pre-scription I can recommend.

A MEDITATION
ON MEDITATION

Each of us, in our own way, is seeking liberation. We want to experience the rapture of reality. We have been taught to pursue this through addition, not subtraction. We think we need to add happiness, prosperity, love, success. However much we add to ourselves, however much we achieve or experience or possess, still we are not whole, and we know it. We can never experience the rapture of reality through addition, because what we want to enhance — our separate self — is that single condition which keeps the rapture of reality away. We only experience the heart-piercing light of reality through subtraction, when "we" disappear, when we empty ourselves of everything, including "us." In this ending of ourself, there is silence. There is love. If "we" do the seeking, if we try to experience the rapture of reality, we will fail. We are in the way. One's own separate self is the barrier to love. One's own separate self is the disappointment, the sadness, that is at the end of each rainbow of hope. We can't do anything about it, because if we do, we will only strengthen an image of "me."

We can only see that the separate self is a facade. When we see through the facade of the separate self, it collapses; it has no support. Meditation is the eye that can see this. Meditation opens the window to the rapture of reality.

At first, meditation is a practice that teaches us to focus our attention on a single point, perhaps the breath or a mantra or the space between two thoughts. As we focus, we are amazed to discover how many thoughts we have. One begins to see that the mind is nothing but thoughts about things and thoughts about thoughts, and thoughts about thoughts about thoughts. In meditation, we can see directly the chaos of the mind as it races without order or purpose from one thing to the next, careening from the past to the future while barely touching the present moment. We also see that all of these thoughts are self-centered; everything we think about, our whole internal experience, is qualified by this central thought, this image of "me."

As we continue to focus the mind on the object of meditation, we begin to observe the stream of thoughts and emotions without getting lost in them. We see that thoughts and emotions arise in numberless waves within the mind. That which observes the play of thoughts is not the mind, but the awareness from which the mind itself is born. We can see that this awareness is qualitatively different than thinking. It has a depth and silence to it. It is not tied to an image of "me." Awareness refers to itself.

We begin to perceive the world, not through our patterns of thinking, but through this awareness, whose integrity is never compromised by thinking. We begin to perceive in silence, without thoughts and images and symbols. Reality is not represented, but emerges directly and immediately in its pristine state. We see thoughts and images arising and subsiding in a vastness about which nothing can be said or known. Our own self-image, our sense of "me," becomes transparent. Suddenly there are no hands to hold anything, no firm ground to stand upon, no "me" to know and worry about.

Meditation opens the window to silence, and in this silence is love. This love dissolves the anxiety of self-centeredness, because the separate self has merged into silence, into love, into the sky of pure awareness. In this awareness, the true Self is liberated from conditions. Rumi tells us that "reality is a rapture that takes you out of form. You are the unconditioned spirit trapped in conditions."

The appearance of this silence marks the end of meditation as a practice and the beginning of meditation as a state of being. It isn't practiced; it isn't attained. It doesn't belong to anyone. We all belong to it.

As this awareness grows within us, we experience peace. Our chronic restlessness subsides. A way of seeing and knowing, different from thinking, is aroused. We might say it is the intuitive umbilical cord to the sacred, a capacity of perception that is wholistic and instantaneous. It is not fragmented and chaotic. We experience directly that we are not our thoughts, but that thoughts occur within us, as clouds appear in the sky.

Each of us longs to be free from all limiting conditions, from compulsive thought and worry, from the disappointment of self-centered pursuits, from the burden of striving for security and happiness. Who hasn't stared out the window and searched the sky for an answer, for a moment of peace? In that moment we are refreshed by the wholeness of the sky which embraces everything. Our breathing becomes deeper. Our thoughts become quiet. It happens to each of us, almost every day. We seem to be searching for something finer, more subtle, than the usual tension and pressure of our lives. A voice we hope to hear. A light we strain to see.

We have to become very still to be able to see and hear and sense this subtlety that we usually glimpse only in rare, unguarded moments. This subtlety is covered by the cacophony of our thoughts. We perceive this subtlety of life, not with thoughts, but with awareness. When we begin to see with subtlety, we begin to sense a pervasive presence, about which nothing can be thought. When we try to know it, it recedes; when we simply allow it to be, it emerges. There's no longing; there's no clinging; there's no struggling; there's no persistent effort. There's simply an opening in which this subtle pervasive presence emerges. Even our thoughts appear in the midst of all of this, but they no longer obscure that presence.

This state of merging with the subtle presence is called natural meditation. Natural meditation is the atmosphere of the sacred hub. It is known in silence. It is who we are. Silence is a release within oneself of all self-centered concern. It is, in fact, death, but a death of smallness, pettiness, and fear. It is the death of the repetitive cycle of desire, fulfillment, and disappointment that is the hallmark of self-centered living.

Meditation dissolves the mental images with which we have identified. Meditation is a fire that consumes the names and forms and conditions with which we have become fascinated. This fascination with the content of the mind creates the sense of being bound and alone and separate. The radiant presence which animates the whole of this universe, the Self, is suppressed by the tyranny of thought. Meditation liberates the Self from its apparent obscurity.

We don't attain anything through meditation. We don't become whole through meditation because we already are whole. Meditation does not fulfill our wishes and dreams: it ends wishing and dreaming. It is the supreme awakening. Meditation reveals the illusion of separation and all of the loneliness and sadness and fear that attend alienation from the Self. Meditation breaks our fascination with the alluring images of the mind. We come to see what those images are and how they come into being. We see this as meditation ripens. We see how all of the effort associated with self-centeredness is so unnecessary and destructive.

Meditation allows us to see that we are not, essentially, defined or limited by our bodies, our minds, or the various patterns through which our senses perceive the external world. We are able to see that we are, essentially, is the hub from which all these forms and ideas arise and around which they revolve. From the sacred hub, we can see a glowing presence, a shimmering light, around everything. This emanation of energy, of presence, of consciousness, saturates each cell, each plant, each mountain, each person, each universe. All of these things are the spokes of the sacred hub, the Self.

This energy of consciousness is revealed in silence, and it is completely beautiful, full of love. In this beauty we fall in love with all things. It is not possessive love. It is not dependent love. It's simply a quality of that consciousness that emerges from silence.

We will never be truly happy unless we return to this source. If we would just sit quietly by the open window of our heart for a few minutes each day, soon the light of that consciousness will be evident.

THE GUILLOTINE
OF SILENCE

The impressions of the mind persist for a long time. The mind is so active, full of false imaginings with which we identify. We can become lost even on our way to the kitchen to get a drink. What do we do? How do we meet our active lives, full of duties and responsibilities and challenges, without losing the clarity and peace of our meditation? We can inquire. We can turn our attention toward the mind and question it. We can face our projections directly, with silent awareness. We can find out what thoughts are, what reactivity is. We can find out what feelings are. We can find out what experience actually is. We can see directly for ourselves what these are and where they come from and where they go to when they are no longer in our awareness. Inquiry prevents the mind from becoming lost in its own projections. Inquiry reveals the mind's anxiety and attachments and denials. In the mirror of persistent questioning, the mind will see its own limitation.

I do not mean that we should think about thoughts or feelings or experience. This gets us nowhere. We inquire into the nature of the mind with awareness. With awareness as our light, we will see the mind's chronic restlessness; we will see its cravings and fear.

Inquiry, like meditation, lures the mind onto the guillotine of silence. The mind is chopped off and falls into the basket of silence, along with the tensions and anxieties of our false imaginings.

WHO AM I?

The root of all inquiry is the question "Who am I?" Under persistent questioning, the mind will not be able to locate itself, its own sense of "I"-ness. When the mind sees for itself that it can't locate — anywhere — who it pretends to be, the habitual patterns of perception associated with our particular "I"-ness disappear in a flash of intuitive awareness.

When Zen master Tokusan had this insight, he threw his treasured copy of the Diamond Sutra, the sacred Buddhist text that he carried everywhere, into a fire. He said, "However deep one's knowledge of abstruse philosophy, it is like a piece of hair flying in the vastness of space; however important one's experience in things worldly, it is like a drop of water thrown into an unfathomable abyss. When insight comes, everyone disappears."

We can never find who we think we are, and yet we go through life so certain that we are something. Everything we do is in some way to enhance, protect, or secure this something that can never be located. This is the root of all delusion, because the "I"-thought is that concept in which all other ideas and concepts find refuge and significance. The unexamined "I"-thought becomes the hallucination called the separate self.

The problems in life that are created by the mind of the separate self — issues of being, of meaning, of inner peace and happiness, of compassionate and intelligent action — can never be resolved by the mind. These things are resolved with insight, when awareness emerges from the jungle of tension and thought. Then the mind will know the peace and security it is always failing to achieve in the outer world.

Ramana Maharshi said, "Self-inquiry leads directly to Self-realization by removing the obstacles which make you think that the Self is not already realized. Whatever be the means adopted, you must at last return to the Self: so why not abide in the Self here and now?"

LIGHT

We have all had the experience that everything is connected to everything else. What is it that binds all things together? It is the light of consciousness, the radiance of the Self.

Twenty years ago, I was living in an ashram in India. One morning, around 5:30, I was leaving the kitchen in which I had been cleaning and cutting fruits and vegetables for the communal lunch. The sun was just rising above the mountain ridge across the valley. I sat on a concrete planter that surrounded several coconut trees and fell very silent.

My head became heavy with silence and my body began to disappear, to dissolve. In another moment there was only breathing, not just my breathing — the respiration of the body — but a breathing of everything around me. I entered that breath of all things and disappeared.

In this breath was a light, a white light. It emanated from everything. It was everywhere. The leaves and flowers of plants, stone walls, the clumps of dirt, the muddy water, the people beginning to pass by — awareness of breathing and light, yet no perceiver, no body, no self. And tremendous order and intelligence! Such precision and purpose — each thing related exquisitely to the next — everything defined within itself and in relation to everything else, ordered and sustained by the breathing and the light which had no source but was everywhere, streaming, busy and yet unmoving.

This lasted for two days, after which I did not want to talk for a long time.

The residue of this experience is with me to this day. I know that I embrace all of life within me, and I am embraced by all of life. Sometimes I cry from the release of tension, when the utter peace of that light returns. I know the world is a condensation of this breath. We are particles of the light of this breath.

It is this light which gives beauty and significance to all things. It is this light which binds everything together. This light is the breath of love. This light is the Self, and it pervades the entire universe.

DON'T TRY TO REMEMBER

A woman said to me that she wanted to remember to access the light she had experienced at the core of her being. She said this light is who she really is.

I asked her why she had to remember who she is. I suggested she stop pretending to be who she isn't, and then she would be free to be who she is. It didn't make sense to me for her to pretend to be who she wasn't, all the while trying to remember who she was.

To remember is to think. Whatever we think we are or think we aren't is still thought. Who we are is not reachable by thought. The light appears when we realize we are not thought.

What's the point of pretending to be who we're not? It's a costume party that leaves everyone in tears.

AWARENESS

A wareness can't be explained. It is neither an object nor an experience. It is that consciousness which pervades every atom in the universe. Awareness is the Self.

We usually perceive with thought and know through memory. In this way the world is nothing but a thought form, a representation of what our senses are able to register and what our minds store in their vaults.

Awareness is the intelligence of the creative energy that gives life and vitality to the cells of the brain. Do you know what thought is? Thoughts are lightening flashes in the brain. Thoughts are electrical impulses that careen through channels in the brain like lightening trying to escape from long corridors. These flashes create impressions that are stored as memory. As long as we are immersed in thoughts and memory, we don't know anything of the real world. In between thoughts, when the brain circuitry is momentarily quiet, a gap exists and in this gap awareness flashes independent of the brain's architecture.

Awareness does not need an instrument like the brain to function. It is inherent in all manifestation. Awareness is the vibration of consciousness itself. This awareness is not bound in any way. It is supremely free and unconditioned.

Awareness is not a power of the mind. Awareness transcends the mind and its projections. The mind merges into its source, disappears, and only awareness remains. The wind cannot be seen, but when the trees begin to sway and the leaves gust in little eddies, we know the wind is about. So it is with awareness.

Awareness is present at all times and in all places. Awareness is the play of consciousness, creating everything, holding everything, dissolving everything. Awareness is consciousness; consciousness is the Self; and we are that Self.

It isn't as remote as it seems. We frequently forget to remember ourself, and still we function and things happen. It is only our identification with our body and senses, our mind and memories, and the objects of the world that prevent awareness from expressing itself through us fully. This is why we meditate.

Meditation unfolds this awareness as it dissolves our habitual identifications with thoughts and images in its great silence. This silence is so beautiful. This silence will support us and guide us. When we need to know something, we will know it. When we need to do something, we will do it. We can remain at peace, knowing that the creative power of the whole universe can speak and act through us at will, without our meddling. When awareness needs to use our mind for a specific purpose, it will do so. We can analyse, plan, organize and make distinctions when these serve some purpose of awareness in this world of duality. When that work is over, we remain still and silent, abiding in the beauty of the Self.

When awareness is free of pollution, it reflects supreme consciousness as a still pond reflects the moon.

RECOGNIZING THOUGHTS

When we do not recognize our thoughts as thoughts, our unconscious mental patterns predominate and rule our behavior. When we are unconscious, we don't really know what we are doing. When we don't know what we are doing, we behave as victims, not of other people or circumstances, but of our own ignorance.

Thought is self-justifying, and survives on explanation and rationalization. Thought cannot see itself. The mind sees only its own projections. This is why we can't see how we are the source of our own problems. We try to solve our problems out there in the world or we try to correct another person's behavior. We often miss the fact that what we see out there in the world or in someone else has its origins in our own mind.

When we are lost in thoughts, there is no seeing, there is only justification. The consequences of our actions will remain invisible. We will see only what we want to see, in spite of the evidence. It is quite possible that our entire species will self-destruct because we won't be able see the impending chaos. The chaos is our own creation.

We must learn to recognize our thoughts, not with other thoughts, but with awareness. Without seeing our own thoughts, we deprive ourselves of the guidance of the Self.

Take a single thought and hold it up to the light of scrutiny as one would hold up a luscious apple of handblown glass to see its inner facets. In this examination, we can come to realize what thoughts are, and that we are different from thoughts.

Then our inner luster will shine, and the chaos will end.

COFFEE MUGS
ARE ALIVE, TOO

A friend was boasting about her ability to produce what she wanted with the power of her thoughts. She said that she recently thought of getting a new coffee mug for work. The next day she found the very one she had imagined sitting on her desk, a gift from a colleague. She thought this proved her point.

I suggested that the coffee mug had created her thought. Why not? Jean Klein once remarked, "Cause and effect are only a way of thinking common to everyday life. All action is brought about by numerous factors, and you are only one of them."

We don't like to hear this, because it disturbs our self-centeredness. We like to believe that we can control everything: if things aren't going our way, all we have to do is develop more psychic or spiritual power to get everything we want.

It is not true that lightening doesn't strike in the same place twice. It strikes in the same place as often as is necessary.

SILENCE

Someone once took a Zen Buddhist monk to hear the Boston Symphony perform Beethoven's Fifth Symphony. The monk's comment was, "Not enough silence!" We should become friends with silence. Silence helps us to see the seductive power of our own justifications — the way we become sure and proud of our ideas and positions, our views and our solutions. Silence is the communion we call love.

Silence is in the heart of all things. We cannot hear silence, we become silence. To become silence, we have to find our way through the narrow gap between two thoughts. Silence also begins in that place where the breath, as it enters us, comes to rest, and from where the breath, as it leaves us, comes from.

In this silence, our ears begin to hear some sounds that are so gossamer, we only intuit their music. Our eyes are startled by each thing as it lives in its own silence. Silence is so fine that even the dance of miniscule insects would seem like the violent roar of a thousand fighter-bombers.

We are embraced by silence, and silence cares for us deeply. In the embrace of silence we sense the essence of living things radiating loudly. We fall into this subtle awareness and are cleansed of bitterness and fear.

In silence, we alternate like a well-timed current between being and non-being, between fullness and emptiness.

In silence, everything just happens, without manipulation, without fear and grasping. But this happening occurs only in silence.

About twenty years ago, I took up the practice of not speaking as a way to encourage inner silence. At first it was very hard, because the talking continued automatically in my head. The words crowded into my mouth; I just wouldn't let them out. After a week or so, I began to notice the thinking and talking. It was as if another person was inside of me. That person just noticed. In this noticing, I became aware of what was otherwise an automatic process of thinking and talking. After another week, that person grew large and encompassing. He was just there, watching and noticing silently. That person was a separate consciousness from mine, noticing, witnessing, silently — without judgment or criticism. It was an awareness that was not me, but included me.

In that silence, I could hear that awareness breathing, purring like a cat. My thinking slowed down, and the crowd of words in my mouth thinned out. I began to feel extremely relaxed, still, and quiet — just like a cat sleeping in the sun. My senses became very acute. I could hear a leaf as it fell in the air. I could feel people approaching before I could see them. I could sense what was about to happen. I could notice the thoughts and impulses arise within me while considering their qualities. This awareness seemed to hold everything within itself, as an ocean holds an infinite variety creatures.

Soon, I couldn't find "me" anywhere. I just disappeared. I had crept into everything, and so "I" became "all." I began to see a soft light surrounding whatever I looked at. Everything seemed linked by this etheric light. The purring breath that I had noticed before was now everywhere. I was mostly aware of the soft light, the purring breath, and an unbreakable stillness.

My teacher, Muktananda, had told me to meditate on the mantra hamsa. He said that hamsa is the vibration of that consciousness which pulsates in every atom of this universe. He said that, by paying attention to the point between the incoming and outgoing breath, or to the space between two thoughts, one could experience the truth of hamsa. He taught that hamsa was the pure vibration of life itself, unconditioned by form or thought, and that it pervaded everything. In my experiment with silence, I must have stumbled into hamsa.

Silence orchestrates life. That music cannot be heard with the ears; it is too subtle, too beautiful. It is experienced in the heart and expressed through being.

DANCING WITH SILENCE

If we act from deep within the inner silence, it is as though we are not acting. It is as though we do not exist, that something more encompassing than our own self acts through us. We don't know how the action arises; it is spontaneous. We don't know where the action will take us; we don't know for sure what kind of flower will grow. We can't know this, because we no longer throw our images into the world. Our images are like bombs that leave craters in reality.

The world and we are one. The same subterranean force that moves through us silently moves through the world, too. That force is alive in each cell, radiating intelligence and strength. That same force holds the spinning planets in their orbits. That force moves us forward, stops us, guides us. Kabir said in one of his poems, "Do you think that the same power that gave you radiance in the womb would abandon you now? It is you who have turned away and walked alone into the dark." To end chaos, to find love, to experience fulfillment, turn back toward the radiance.

We are in the silence that gives radiance to life. We need not even recognize this, because this is true whether we see it or not. If, however, we want to end conflict and sorrow, we should find a way to see this for ourselves. We would see that what we are looking for in the world of objects, in the imaginary world of the future, in the perfection of relationships and the pride of achievement, is already present within us. It is resting quietly and serenely beneath the mind that has turned away from silence.

We ask questions with the hope that the answers will bring about some change in us. We hope that to know something will enrich our experience of this moment. But does an answer ever satisfy, fully and totally? Does an answer bring peace, does an answer bring about freedom from stress and agitation and conflict? Have any answers yet put an end to the chaos? Does knowing something with the mind cause love to exist? The mind that wants answers that can be put like apples in a basket will never find fulfillment or peace. Turn over the basket and the mind will fall into the silence beneath it.

DESIRE IS A DEAD END

Desire is a hard road that goes nowhere. And yet we travel on this road, day after day, year after year. Where are we going? Have you ever experienced the promise of desire?

Desire is neither bad nor good; it's just not going to do the trick in the long run. What we need to see is that when we attain the object of our desire, the joy we experience is not in what we have attained. It is the sudden and total lack of desire. The object does not contain the ecstasy; the ecstasy is in the freedom from wanting. Fulfillment in freedom is corrupted by desire. Desire obstructs happiness because what we are looking for cannot be found in the fulfillment of desire. That's all. All desire is compensatory: we crave because we are not full.

A client once told me, "I have everything: a beautiful wife, two wonderful kids, a growing company, two houses and plenty of cars. I have everything I thought I was supposed to have to be happy. I'm not. It's killing me." Building a personal empire based on desire will never liberate the freedom of the Self from our dream of separation.

If we trace to its source the joy we feel upon the fulfillment of desire, we will see that the joy is not in the object; it is inherent within us and is revealed in the freedom from desire. Nisargadatta Maharaj said, "Don't be afraid of a life beyond fear and desire." Imagine, even for a moment, what your life would be like if you were totally free of all desire and longing because you were completely fulfilled in wholeness. We don't really have a clue, do we?

Desire imprisons us in becoming. Mired in the insufficiency of our separateness from life, we fight and struggle to overcome our alienation through becoming. Become secure. Become powerful.

Become loved. But all of our attainments in this world of becoming, fueled by desire, have a shadow, the shadow of a weird failure. They're never quite enough. These attainments are only for the sake of the mind. The mind will never be satisfied, we will never experience peace.

The mind is a bundle of thoughts. Thought is always about something; in this way the mind literally creates the world of duality.

Duality means two: subject and object, perceiver and perceived, experienced and experiencer, desire and object of desire. The fundamental thought that maintains duality is "I," the subject, the experiencer, the perceiver, the one who desires. This sense of duality leads to desire.

We know that we contain all of life within our own Self. We know that we are living in a single field of consciousness, which expresses itself in a kaleidoscope of ways and forms. Desire, the grasping hands of the mind of the separate self, doesn't know this. It perceives the infinite variety of expressions of the Self as separate and different from itself. We can only desire that which is different than we are.

Desire is marbled with attachment, fear, anxiety. When we achieve what we desire, we move on to another desire. There is no end, there is no peace, there is no openness and grace. For these to happen, we have to rest in the Self.

We are afraid of what will happen to us without the pressure of our desires creating our life. We are uncertain about our well-being. Am I not entitled to a prosperous life style? What's wrong with wanting to have a nice home, fashionable clothes, disposable income? Nothing at all. We should all have a good life.

However, most of what we pursue is to compensate for an insecurity in living, an inner poverty of happiness. Our one true desire is to eradicate our sense of separateness, which is the cause of our pain and inner poverty. This is the true desire behind all of our chronic wanting and craving. We can't gather up in our arms everything that is separate from us, we can't collect every experience or sensation it is possible to have. We don't have to build an empire; the empire is already ours.

With everything ours in the empire of the Self, another movement begins to appear, deep within us, and it is this movement that shows us the way. It is a throb, a divine throb, a gentle push of the Self, the pure impulse of the creative energy of the universe. We aren't afraid of what we will or won't have or experience. We don't have to tear at life anymore, fighting to get what we want. What we really want, we already have. When we experience that we already have what we most want, we experience an earthquake of restfulness. The aftershocks are wonderful, tremendous. We never really have to think about ourselves again. The divine throb, the pulsation of the Self, will use us, move us, make us do what we must do. We don't have to make our life turn out, we won't be able to stop it.

We can sit in an easy chair in the observation lounge of the speeding train of the Self. At the right time, we'll be called down for lunch. Later, we'll go to sleep. When we wake up, something will tell us what, if anything, we need to do. But the doing will come through us, without effort and compensation, as waves arise in an ocean.

When the mind is quiet, when the hands of desire are not grabbing and pushing and tearing, the natural order prevails. In the natural order, each thing glows with the sacred aura of its creator. We participate in this order, with appreciation of its beauty. Living in a world of beauty, with each thing sacred, we are at peace.

THIRTY POUNDS
OF POTATOES

If you think about it, you'll see that our greatest joy occurs when we have forgotten about ourselves. I'm not implying that we should become unconscious; I mean that our relationship to life should not be bound by self-centeredness. We come into our true Self when the separate self is absent. Jean Klein said that "in our absence is our presence." This would seem unbelievable, except that we all know it's true.

In our absence, we are taken by something of which we are a part, but which we cannot claim as our own, because we would inevitably want to use it for our own small purposes. We might want to put it outside our house to increase its value. We might wear it as a cologne or perfume to increase our allure and attractiveness. When we claim as our own that into which our separate self merges, we are once again living in false imaginings. We can't willingly give ourselves away; we will always want to remain as a point of reference. Our absence happens only by accident. But in those happy accidents, we discover our true joy and peace.

When we laugh, when we love, when we walk in the woods, at these times we enter the presence of our absence. We are ravished by the simple beauty of life. We are not bothered by our own heaviness, which we normally carry around like thirty pounds of potatoes.

We often make our lives difficult and awkward, as though we were actually carrying around thirty pounds of potatoes. Try it, even for a day. You'll be very relieved when you put the potatoes down. You'll be able to live with more grace and ease. You'll wonder why we ever thought carrying around thirty pounds of potatoes was a good idea.

The only way we can court our own absence is to become sick and tired of carrying around thirty pounds of potatoes. When we see how useless it is, the extra weight falls away by itself. We can't do anything about it. We just have to see it, clearly and totally.

FINDING THE EGO

Does anyone know what the ego is? Whatever is said about the ego becomes food for itself. The ego is self-justifying to the bitter end. The problems of the ego persist.

The ego is a concept, and yet it is real. While it is real, we cannot find it anywhere. It is like quicksand; no matter what we do or which way we move, we sink deeper. If we do nothing, we'll also sink deeper. Nothing can be said to change this.

We must do something, and yet there is nothing we can do. Still, we cannot give up.

Live with this, and see what happens. In living with this, try to find the ego, try to see it, face to face. Don't try to know something about it, try to find it. But know that whatever you find, behind that is more ego, feeling proud and taking credit for having found something. Be especially careful of discovering egolessness, because that is ego in drag. Continue to struggle, don't give up, and know there is nothing you can do. Whatever you find, know that the ego has found it. Whatever is not found, the ego has not found it.

Be careful also when you hear that one perfectly exquisite and definitive explanation and remedy. The ego says it, the ego hears it, the ego knows it. The ego smiles in self-satisfaction.

Don't give up. If you do, it is the ego that gives up. If you don't, it is the ego that doesn't. Just try to see it, face to face. Be committed to this, even though it is the ego's commitment. Try with all your might to find it. Give every bit of your strength to find it.

Meditate, turn within, sit in silence. Continue in this way to find it, to see it. Inquire, examine, go deep. Try to locate it.

One day the ego will not be a problem, but "you" won't ever know it.

THE PERSISTENCE OF EGO

The ego is like the cockroach: resilient and persistent beyond rea-son. We have set many traps for the ego, but it is only strength-ened by those efforts. What are we to do?

Nothing. Nothing at all. Anything that can be done will be done by the ego itself. Action will only breed more ego, more cockroaches. If one would like to be free from the pains of the ego, simply notice it. Become aware of what it is. And do nothing. Just notice.

What is the ego? The ego is a thought pattern that creates and projects the feeling of a separate person on to the screen of reality. The ego is an habitual hallucination. This thought pattern obscures reality. Reality appears when that particular thought pattern is dis-rupted. As long as the ego persists, our lives are expressions of our desires and fears. Desire and fear are the two sides of the ego. Both conditions are symptoms of unreality. The ego is a wall of thought that blocks reality. Notice this. See how the ego operates. This seeing is the only action, really a non-action, that will rid us of this pain.

Desire is the aspect of ego that seeks the security of eternal life. Our desires aim to enhance and decorate the separate self. Look at your own life. Examine desire itself. Do not label it good or bad, but just see what desire is and how it affects you.

Fear is the aspect of ego that seeks to protect and preserve the separate self. Look at what fear is, see what it does. The ego is a thought pattern that is sustained through the secondary thoughts of desire and fear. As long as we live through the ego, we will have this context imbedded within us.

This is why it is so hard to bring about change in ourselves or in the world. We have not changed the context in which our experience arises. Everything we do is an attempt to fulfill desire or to mitigate fear. We don't remove the cataracts from our eyes. Throughout our history, only a handful of people have done this. We call them mystics, saints, or sages. The rest of us accord them great esteem because something in us knows how true they are, and through them we have tasted a drop of that silent reality we know as love. A drop of the true life lingers on our tongues.

Our greatest challenge is to overcome this idea of the ego. Even as I write this I am noticing how unthinkable it is, and yet I remember a line from Rumi, "Start a huge, foolish project, like Noah did. It makes absolutely no difference what people think of you."

We think that our planning and our effort and our striving is what makes things happen and what secures our future. We don't see the big picture that the poet Issa saw when he wrote, "Simply trust. Do not the petals flutter down, just like that?" It is difficult to see the details of our lives occurring in the same natural, simple manner.

Nisargadatta Maharaj remarked, "Do not be afraid of freedom from desire and fear. It enables you to live a life so different from all you know, so much more interesting and intense, that by losing all, you gain all." It is too implausible to consider that we ourselves are the barrier to real fulfillment in life. We have so little knowledge of how life unfolds on the other side of desire and fear.

Every once in a while, the ego disappears. For a moment we see. Something marvelous occurs. We are delighted when we suddenly break free and forget ourselves and our habitual desires and fears, our prejudice and striving. We become aware of light, silence, and joy. These belong to no one. These just are. Life is there in all its immediacy and fullness. We return to our natural state. We are no longer afraid of the life on the other side of our imaginary self's death. A Zenrin poem says, "Sitting quietly, doing nothing, Spring comes, and the grass grows by itself."

THERE IS NO
SPIRITUAL LIFE

There is no such thing as a spiritual life.

Spiritual practices are designed to affect the mind, to purify it and make it capable of perceiving subtlety. There are many systems of practice. All of these practices prepare the mind to meet and recognize the Self. In this recognition, the separate self dissolves.

These practices can become a source of fascination for the ego. The ego is a magician at claiming ownership. "This is mine!" insists the ego, the "I"-thought. Once we begin these practices, once we begin to have certain experiences, the "I"-thought within us begins to think, I have become spiritual.

The "I"-thought, cloaking itself in spirituality, now has a whole new set of self-justifications and rationalizations for itself. It labels new experiences "nonordinary," "altered," "mystical," or "transcendent." All of this is from the perspective of the separate self.

Has one yet come face to face with the truth of one's own life? Has one seen how quickly and absolutely the ego appropriates that which is beyond itself? Until this "I"-thought has been seen and unmasked, our reference point will be the same. The only difference is the spin we put on it, the new experiences and insights we have.

The only entity that can experience a "spiritual" life or experience is the mind. From the perspective of life itself, there is neither spiritual nor non-spiritual. There is simply life as it is: vast, evolving, multi-dimensional. The "miracles" attributed to great masters and healers and that can occur to many of us in everyday life are not based in a rarefied spiritual world. They are the way things work, naturally. If we live in a crude world, then we have turned a blind eye to what life is.

When the mind appropriates the residue of silence to itself as an experience, the problem of the spiritual ego begins. This is when people try to "use" spirituality to enhance their life or to correct some injustice in the world. This never works, because the mind that created the imbalance is again at the controls, only this time with a different rationale, a different cloak of righteousness. Do not confuse this with a spiritual life. It has only to do with the life of the ego. As long as there is even the faintest smell of "I," the ego is at play.

In order to unmask the "I"-thought, we must see ourselves honestly and clearly, without any rationalization or self-interest. We must want only to see. We must not care at all for results or outcomes. We must not care at all, not in the least, what happens to us, to our own life. We must care only for an honest, direct, undistorted seeing of our actions. When this happens, we will instantly see what our motives are. In seeing our motives, we will see the "I"-thought. In seeing the "I"-thought, all motives dissolve in the seeing of the single motive which supports all other motives: "me." When this is seen, one becomes free. One does not become a spiritual "me" or a "not-me." One becomes what one is, the essence, free from motive, played upon by life, carried by life.

When one is played upon by life, one can only respond with what life is. Life is not vicious, cruel, violent, greedy. These responses are the responses of the "I"-thought, whether spiritualized or not, because its sole motive is to persist. To persist, it must become stronger, craftier, more devious.

That which is true can't be named; therefore, remain silent. Just be silent. This silence will cause a transformation of behavior as it dissolves the spiritual ego.

One need only find the source of the root delusion of the mind, the "I"-thought. Whatever happens on the other side of that discovery cannot be described, labeled, or categorized. If we are concerned with spiritualizing our life, we will not find this out, because the ego, whether spiritual or not, will never approve its own death.

Muktananda put this quite simply, "When the ego dies, God arises." The spiritual ego dissolves over time as we continue to go deep within ourselves through the inner silence and power of meditation.

INFLATING
OUR OWN BALLOON

Self-importance is the air that inflates the balloon of our own destruction. The larger we become, the closer we are to bursting.

When we do things to expand the feeling of being a separate self, our pride expands also. Pride is a badge of honor for the separate self. However, as our pride expands, so does the belief in our separate self. The appetite of pride is never satisfied. Once we start feeding it, we must feed it forever.

Pride and anger are close relatives. Hostility and violence are cousins. Think about it. When someone sticks a pin in our pride, we become angry. As our anger swells, we want to strike out at the pin that burst our balloon of self-importance.

Sometimes our pride conceals itself behind a screen of unimportance. That is really false humility — a huge, hot-air balloon.

If we could see that the furtive movement of the separate self is a false imagining, we would stop blowing up the balloon of our own destruction. We would see that, while nothing is important, everything is sacred.

Become a servant of the sacred.

PURSUING RELATIONSHIPS

We often enter relationships without knowing our own Self, hoping that another person will provide what we think we don't already have.

We create an image of ourselves that reflects our incompleteness, and we hold out that image to another person. They, in turn, hold out their image to us. The relationship begins, but it is a relationship of two images, two objects, two sets of desires. This kind of relationship ends in disappointment because it is not authentic. We might blame some discrepancy of compatibility or life purpose, but, in reality, the disappointment is that neither has been touched. Only the images are touched. This collision of images creates the patterns in our relationships, and it is the reason we often feel that we come to the same end, only with different people.

What is our motive for pursuing relationships? Is it to provide security — financial, emotional, psychological? Is it to mitigate loneliness or boredom? Is it to dramatize our own need to dominate and control? Is it to animate deep-seated fantasies and imaginings? Is there a strong sexual urge that demands consummation without regard to the consequences?

When we look at another person, what do we see? Do we see only an object to satisfy our unexamined needs, desires, and fantasies? And if we say that we do see another person, are we seeing only the facade of their projected imagination and cravings?

We cannot pursue other people as prey. In doing so, there is always deception and sadness. The unexamined desires behind "pursuing" relationships are never fulfilled.

There are some people with whom we experience an instant

magnetism that is overwhelming. We feel deep currents of attraction and love. We immediately channel this energy of attraction into the trap of our fantasies. Think how often our response to attraction is, "This is the one!" We are not meant to possess the object of our love, to imprison it in our wanting. Only in freedom is there love. When we experience love with someone, it is to deepen our capacity for love.

We must be honest about our motives for "pursuing" relationships. If we hope that another person will fill us with what we don't already have, we are sowing the seeds of attachment and dependency. First, we have to know what we are missing; we have to know what it is that we want another person to fulfill for us. Once we see this clearly, we might also see that it is our responsibility to fulfill ourselves with our own inner resources of being and Self-knowing. Having done this, we can bring this fullness to every person we meet. We can meet others with openness, with patience, with discernment. This openness of being allows us to truly discover another person's essence, to touch and be touched deeply, without desperation, without need.

If we are more restrained, initially, we can allow the proper unfolding of a relationship. We won't be bothered by the hungry urgency of our projected images. We can enjoy being together with others in the spirit of freedom. We can let things develop. As we move in the world, without desperation, without hunger, we will meet many people. We will have many relationships, some of which might last for a day, others deep and enduring.

Let people enter your life freely, with ease and happiness and respect. Don't treat them as objects, but discover them with openness and curiosity. Don't become agitated and tense. Don't grab, don't hold on. Stay balanced in your own Self.

We don't have to ruin each other over and over again, as we do when we try to lure another into the trap of our inner emptiness. Pursue your own Self, and then let everything else pursue you.

INTIMACY

Many people are disappointed in their relationships because they can't achieve a certain "something" with their partner. This "something" is often called intimacy. When we don't experience this intimacy with another, we say it is because one or the other or both have "problems with intimacy." Then we find out why, and try to correct, adjust, or heal the "why" in order to experience more intimacy.

What is intimacy? What is the feeling we want intimacy to create? Do we feel somehow disconnected from others, from ourselves, from life? Is intimacy the answer to loneliness and isolation?

We do not feel intimacy when we share the events of our life. This only familiarizes us with the elements of another's personal history, compiled and edited and revised by them. We are not fulfilled through our stories, because we can connect only with our remembered past and anticipated future. We are not the past; we are not the future.

Intimacy occurs when our minds are still and our hearts are open, when we relate authentically, without rehearsed messages of past conditioning. When we face life with the mask of our past, is there any real connection with others, or is there only disappointment and emptiness?

Intimacy is the experience of love as it moves out from our center into the world around us. We say we experience intimacy with another person, but if we look carefully we see that what we call intimacy is the experience of letting our love out, indiscriminately. Letting our love out is fulfillment in itself. Intimacy describes the state of joining with life when we forget ourselves. Intimacy is fulfilled when we allow our original innocence to emerge, when we don't project the past and when we don't hold ourselves in.

What are we? Are we an isolated person, an object, roaming in a world of other objects? Can two objects ever merge in a true union, or does true union, true intimacy, occur when all ideas of self and other are abandoned? Can there be intimacy between two people, or does intimacy refer to a oneness, a wholeness of being that is not related to our ideas, our desires, or our loneliness?

Intimacy cannot be practiced or achieved. We are already connected, essentially, to every other living thing. We have covered our own innocence with pain and fear. We have become suspicious and cautious. Isn't this true? We approach each other with calculators, like actuaries, weighing perceived risks and benefits. We are poised to attack and conquer, or to retreat and protect. Our past makes us suspicious, our suspicions make us anxious, and our anxiety reinforces our suspicions.

The separate self can never experience true intimacy. Intimacy is transparency of living: to touch and be touched by life with an openness and a freshness that is uncorrupted by the past and the future. If one wants to experience intimacy, one must retrieve one's own original Self, one must recover one's innocence from behind the mask of our practiced isolationism.

LONELINESS

We do not enjoy loneliness, do we? When we feel alone, we become agitated or depressed. We will do anything to keep our minds from experiencing loneliness. We'll call a friend, turn on the television, pick up a book, or start cleaning the garage. These are not in and of themselves bad things to do. It's just that if we do these things to avoid the experience of being lonely, we will always be plagued by it, and our resistance to and avoidance of loneliness will increase over time. We will try to stay one step ahead of it, like racing down a mountain slope in front of an avalanche.

That's why we make loneliness a problem; we stay out in front of it, trying to avoid being touched by it. Whenever we sense it creeping into our awareness, we start to feel bad: nervous, fearful, angry, frustrated. We don't really want to experience any of these either. Watch what happens.

We do something to dissipate the nervousness, fear, or frustration. As long as we are engaged in the activity that suppresses the symptoms of loneliness, we think we are not lonely. This is not true. We have only avoided seeing what loneliness is. It will return. And everything we do to suppress the symptoms of loneliness will make us feel even more lonely.

What are the subtle movements within us that give rise to what we call loneliness? Do we want to know? Are we willing to find out?

Loneliness is itself a symptom of living in the dualism of conventional reality. We believe we live in a world of objects, that we are but an isolated planet spinning in the incomprehensible vastness of intergalactic space. It is cold in space. We can go for years and years without making contact with another object. When we finally connect with another object, we hold tight; we won't let go. This is called attachment. Objectification and attachment feed the experience of loneliness.

Still, this is explanation, not seeing. One must see for oneself how loneliness comes into being from subtle movements within one's own consciousness. How can you see this? Stop running. Stay put. Sit down. Turn around and face loneliness.

Sit down, be quiet, and face loneliness. Don't be intimidated by its symptoms. Walk through them, as through a fog. Walk through loneliness, too, with your inner eyes. Its only a mirage; you can never actually come upon it. Loneliness is a ghost of objectification and attachment; both of which obscure who you are.

Who are you? You will find out when you walk through loneliness, when you walk through fear and nervousness and the imaginary cold eternal space of objects. Walking through loneliness, you dissolve yourself as an object. Dissolving yourself as an object, you dissolve the world of objects. When the world of objects disappears, the world of consciousness, of the Self, appears.

When the Self appears, even the molecules of air become good companions. The curtains, the hardwood floor, plants growing in the clay pots on the deck all reflect something not seen in the world of objects. A soft light, the breathing of life, speech and thought of a different order. How can one be lonely in a sea of consciousness in which one's own sense of being an object is dissolved?

Can you see this for yourself? Can you see that your loneliness is a symptom of objectifying yourself, and that when you turn and walk through loneliness you enter the world of the Self?

In the world of the Self, objects appear against the background of silence and consciousness from which they come. When the silence and consciousness of the Self are liberated from the world of objects, there is no one to feel lonely!

LOVE IS OUR ESSENCE

Love cannot be found, for love is not an object. Love is our essence, and it is only revealed when we stop relating to ourselves and others as objects. Love can never be attained. The disappointment that we feel in not having found the love we want is not a defect of love, but of our approach.

Love wants us, too. Love needs to be expressed through us, but it must wait until we have shaken everything that we think has love in it. Love must wait until we have become exhausted and supremely disappointed in our search to find love where it isn't. Then it appears.

Love is not a business. We can't make a deal for love; we can't hope to have love just because we sign on the dotted line of a contract. Love comes by itself when we stop wanting, when wanting is exhausted. In that moment, we become the love that we have been hoping to find.

The love we are seeking is always stalking us. It is never far from where we are right now. We are looking in the wrong direction. Become silent. Become still. In this silence love appears.

Don't settle for security. That is not love. Don't settle for getting what you want. That is not love. Don't settle for flattery or fleeting pleasure. Love is deep and lasting. But it can't be found. It can't be won, like a prize. We have to see that it is already there within us. We must first find it where it is, and then we will see it everywhere.

Love is not a trap we set for the unsuspecting. Love is not imprisoning others in our self-centered fantasies. Love is a profound caring for life, and all of its expressions. Love always takes us out of ourself and into the Self. Real love is rare, because the price of love is everything we want, everything we hope for. Wanting and hoping keeps the objective world alive, and where the objective world is alive, love is not. Only when all objects and ideas of self and others have merged into the Self can love appear. We do not need to cling tightly to the imagined objects of our love.

The greatest gift we can give someone we love is the gift of their freedom from our attachment. Don't waver. Don't be held back by attachments, by fears. It seems hard to do. It is, at first, but then love itself gives us more than we could ever have imagined. Love gives us freedom, and in this freedom we are love, and wherever we turn, whatever we do, we give love, and in giving love, we receive the love that we are.

Throw yourself into the ocean of the Self with ruthless finality. The love that is found in the Self leads us ever deeper into love. Be still, be silent, be carried away by the deep currents moving right now within you. The Self is an ocean of infinite love.

HEALING THE PAST

The past is not always with us. There are moments when the past is consumed by love, which is the intoxication of our natural state. What we remember about the past is not our natural state. Fundamentally, we are not that which can be conditioned by memory, by the past, by time. It is important to see that a part of us is already healed; in fact, a part of us is not capable of being wounded. If we don't start from this insight, we will always fall back into the mire of the past. We have all sustained too many wounds to heal them all, one at a time. As long as we continue to identify with our separate self, we will experience the sorrow of past sufferings.

What is it exactly we want to heal? Perhaps, as a child, we were terrified by something cruel or violent. Perhaps we were personally violated, physically, emotionally, or mentally. Maybe no one loved us, or received our love. There are so many ways in which the thudding hammer blows of ignorant behavior can terrify us. Who hasn't experienced some of this? So much of life is one disappointment after another. We are criticized. We are told many negative things about ourselves, all of it false, but we absorb it and belief it. We experience shame and embarrassment. We begin to feel small and distrustful of ourselves, and so we hold back. Our spirit shrinks, and we begin to live in tiny rooms, in attics and basements, in shadows and darkness and fear.

These impressions take on full lives within us. Through the filters of these impressions, we meet each new situation as if it were the old one, and we prepare for the worst. This is the way that old wounds deprive us of the experience of our spirit, of our true Self. We dread the past and yet, without knowing it, we throw it out be-

fore us, seeding the future with the past. This is the source of the
heaviness, the disappointment, the sadness that follows us from one
day to the next. The old wounds suck out from the marrow of our
lives the very joy and spaciousness of free living.

To heal this damage of abuse is necessary for our emotional
and psychological well-being and happiness. But even as we under-
take this healing work, we may find that the roots of our suffering
do not originate in adolescence, or childhood, or even in this life.
The original damage may have occurred in a previous life. We may
find that it is difficult to pinpoint the specific time and perpetrator
of our wound. The terrain in which we search for clues to our pain is
really a vast wilderness, a journey that may take us into the distant
past of forgotten lifetimes.

As we travel deeply into this healing process, we begin to see
recurring themes, recurring situations, recurring relationship patterns. One begins to wonder who, in fact, does what to whom. The
tremendous wheel of life has been turning for eons. We have been
many things, done many things, known many people. We need to
find a high ground of insight to know the truth of our lives, and of
how and why things happen the way they do.

I think that all of the suffering that we experience and inflict
comes from a fundamental wound that is common to all of us. That
wound is the separation from our source within consciousness itself. We must return to our original Self, through meditation,
through prayer, through silent inquiry. As we do this, the energy of
the Self is liberated, bit by bit. The inner energy that is activated
through meditation will cause these old wounds to come out of the
shadows and into the light. Some will disappear in the first seeing.
Other impressions might need to be worked with, to be coaxed fully
out of their hiding. When this is necessary, we will see that some
person or resource becomes available to us. Just be open to this as-
sistance appearing.

We should be careful not to become addicted to the healing
work itself. The way to heal the past is to see that the wounds and
impressions of the past are not who we are. We don't need to revel
in what is essentially not real. We don't have to assemble a new

false self to counteract the old false self. Any self-image, whether of a shamed and embarrassed child or of a strong and fearless adult, misses the mark of who we really are. Let us do what work is necessary and be done with it. It isn't necessary to create a detailed understanding of the past, for this kind of knowing does not free us. Let the old impressions surface naturally, see them totally with complete openness, and let them go. It's not necessary to rewrite our whole personal history, which is already too extensive.

I think the best way to begin to heal our wounds is to connect with that part of ourselves that can never be wounded. Become silent inside, and let that silence begin to wash the old hurts. The true healing is from a recognition that who we are is vast, untrammeled, not spoiled by the past. The essential Self, the eternal flame of the divine, is already healed because it can never be wounded. By contacting this Self first, that very thing which is wounded begins to dissolve, along with its millions of impressions.

EATING COSMIC DUST

We are confused about who we are. We usually think we are everything that has ever happened to us. Without considering it, we attach ourselves to thoughts and feelings and experiences, as barnacles attach themselves to the hulls of ships.

Our attachments become our identity. Our identity is who we think we are. We walk around as though we were the sum total of all the thoughts and feelings we have ever experienced. From this perspective, our personal history is very important and defining. From the perspective of the universe, our identities are invisible specks of cosmic dust.

We are not what we think we are. We are not barnacles feeding off the hull of memory. We are the Self, and the Self eats and digests two hundred trillion specks of cosmic dust every second.

MEDITATION IN DAILY LIFE

The peace that we experience in meditation cannot be carried into our daily life. That peace is who we are, and therefore it cannot be carried anywhere. We can only carry something that we are not. The peace of meditation is already present wherever we are. The question is, Why don't we experience that?

The practice of meditation is not the source of the peace we feel, it reveals the peace that is already within us. The peace that is within us is revealed when we turn our attention inward. In meditation we withdraw our attention from the chaos of the world and we stop projecting the fantasies of our mind. Then, without the mind of the world and the world of the mind to distract us, who we are emerges.

As we experience more of who we are, the peace of that Self-knowledge follows us everywhere. We can't escape it. Don't try to bring that peace anywhere. Just find out who you are.

Return to silence as often as you can. Without clinging to your ideas and plans, without resisting natural changes, let this silence begin to shape your life, and as it does you will experience the peace you want.

This silence, this energy of meditation, will carry us. We can't carry it.

AMUSEMENT PARKS

The present moment is always here; where are you? When you are not present, where exactly do you go?

In school, my teachers took roll call to see who was in class. We were expected to say "present." If we did not respond, we were thought to be elsewhere. If the teacher saw that we were in class but did not say "present," the roll call stopped until we became present enough to say "present."

Sometimes when I was in class, I didn't say "present." Where was I? I was in the amusement park of my mind.

The mind is full of exciting rides. Some are fun. Some are scary. Others leave us in a sentimental mood. However, none of the rides are here, where the teacher is waiting.

The mind swings in great unstoppable arcs from the past to the future. The mind can never be present. The mind can only see the present in its rear-view mirror, because the present is too real and immediate.

For the mind, the present is just another idea, another concept. The mind creates representations of reality; it can never grasp reality because reality itself is too subtle.

Only when we leave the amusement park of our mind can we enter reality.

BEING MINDFUL

What does it mean to be mindful? Being mindful means that we are alert to what is happening within us and around us as it is occurring. It means that our mind is clear and our senses open, that we are responding effectively and creatively to what is at hand, without thinking about it. It is an immediacy of experience, a direct connection with the freshness of each new moment. We feel each breath as it enters us, and we feel each breath as it leaves us. We are conscious of each bite and chew of our food. We are as sensitive to the nuances of life around us as we are to the arising thoughts and feelings within us. This is being mindful.

Being mindful and attentive to what is occurring now is extremely useful for dealing effectively with our daily lives. It is also a good practice for spiritual development. Mindfulness produces the feeling of being centered and balanced.

To practice mindfulness, we focus and concentrate the mind on a single point. Concentration on a single point helps us to free ourselves from the mind's eccentricities.

But mindfulness is still self-centered. The feeling of being centered and balanced belongs to us. It is another state, localized in space and time. It helps us, but it is not who we are. In order to be truly free, mindfulness must grow into awareness.

Mindfulness means to be alert to the here and now of this physical environment. It is the quality of mind in its pristine state. This mind is cultivated through attention and dis-identification with thought. This mind sees things as they are, without embellishment or added significance.

Awareness, however, is more encompassing than mindfulness.

Awareness is the subtle consciousness that is the animating force of the mind. It is not related to the past or the future. It is not related to the present. It is beyond all three.

Awareness does not belong to us, as does mindfulness. Awareness is beyond a practicer. Awareness is like a gust of insight whose source is beyond knowing. Awareness is not a state of mind; it is a quality of being. This beingness is beyond conditions. In this awareness, one does not have to worry about being centered in the present.

As mindfulness matures into awareness, our sense of being a separate self dissolves. This dissolution allows awareness to emerge within us. As this awareness emerges from the shadows cast by our own separateness, the effort and striving to be present also dissolve.

When the separate self merges back into awareness, everything is seen as an expression of life, of consciousness, of the Self. Here, in the sacred hub, differences of name and form and experience lose their distinctive edge. Around the now-soft edges is the shimmering light of consciousness itself. We do not need caution or alertness, because in this ocean of consciousness everything is wet. But we must experience this, we must know this, we must make this real. We cannot sit on the shore and think we know what it's like to be in the ocean.

TWO KINDS OF CHANGE

We confuse the change we try to impose on life and the change life imposes on us. The changes we try to impose are spasms of the mind. The spasms of the mind are always at odds with life. The conflict grows into the chaos we can see all around us. This chaos is not natural. The more threatening the chaos becomes, the more we impose our will on it, trying to direct it away from us. But we created the chaos by not understanding the difference between the two kinds of change.

The change that life imposes on us is called impermanence. Understanding and accepting impermanence brings us closer to reality and opens us to a life of humility. This humility is a deep spiritual peace. When we allow life to carry us along, the changes are organic and help us grow in our understanding and experience of life itself. As humility and peace deepen within us, we are guided by a correctness of choice and action. Without fear, we can allow what must pass away to pass away. Security is provided by life as its mystery is played out through us. Something new will always be born and life itself is the midwife.

There is a poignancy in the recognition of impermanence, and our heart will often feel pierced by the passing away of what we have loved. But it is this very poignancy that helps us to open to each other with love and compassion, because each moment may be the last moment. Why spend it in anger? Why be critical of ourselves and others? Should we not spend each moment, knowing it may be our last, in forgiveness and love?

If we become close to the earth and her seasons, we will be reminded of life's changes. If we contemplate our own body, we will see that it is in a state of constant change and reflects the cycle of all living things: birth, growth, decay, and death. This is impermanence. Shouldn't we live in accord with this law?

The recognition of impermanence allows us to be open to the poignant beauty of each moment, and we will be able to touch each task, each person, each living thing with love and appreciation.

The more we try to impose our will on life, the more estranged we become from the harmony of the Self.

IMPERMANENCE

There is one thing that we can count on in life, and that is impermanence. Everything that exists is in a constant state of passing away. There is nothing we can do to change this. Impermanence is an indisputable fact of life, but we behave as though it isn't.

Have you ever built a sand castle by the seashore? It's easy to get caught up in designing and building it. We forget to cast an eye toward the inevitable. At a certain time the tide begins to come in, whether we are finished or not, whether we want it to nor not. Regardless of our plans and calculations, the tide will come in at the appointed hour and it will wash our castle out to sea. I think we get caught up in designing and building our lives, too. If we ignore the fact of the tide, we will certainly experience suffering and disappointment. If we understand the fact of impermanence, we can can live more fully in the depth and beauty of each moment, without clinging, without resisting.

The more we cling to our desires, the harsher impermanence feels. The more we resist impermanence, the more afraid we become. Our fear is rooted in a denial of the basic fact of life.

Behind most of our desires is the desire for security. We want things to be certain and to last. They aren't and they don't. The more we impose our desire for security onto life, the more we experience insecurity, because our conflict with life increases. We have not seen this clearly; we have not accepted this. An intellectual understanding of impermanence is not enough. We have to give our lives to the truth of impermanence and learn to live fully even as its frothy tide constantly washes over our feet.

There is no firm ground to stand on. There are no legs to stand with. When we see this, our conflict with life will end. Our fear will end. We will be free to love deeply each person, each thing, each moment as it appears and disappears according to the sacred scriptures of impermanence.

HAPPINESS

We do everything for the sake of happiness. In spite of this, it eludes us. Happiness is fleeting and unpredictable. Even when we think we have happiness firmly in hand, we can't hold it for long. Our very efforts to achieve happiness often seem to produce frustration, anger, and sadness.

What is happiness? Do we mean security? The fulfillment of desires? Some form of excitement? The attention of a lover? The approval of our parents? Do we really know what is meant by happiness?

Happiness is not something in and of itself. We cannot pursue it; we cannot achieve it; we cannot possess it. Rather, happiness refers to a state of being that occurs automatically in the absence of self-concern. This happiness is not achieved. It simply is. This happiness is revealed as a part of life in its wholeness, its totality. We can't experience this happiness as a thing which can be sought and found. It is already there, as a fact of living. We have to see what we do to obscure the happiness that is unconditionally present within us.

The person seeking happiness will never find it. What the person seeking happiness will find is a mirage, temporary and conditioned by circumstances. When circumstances change, they will again experience anxiety and emptiness. The search for happiness begins again.

We want to find happiness, but it is not an object. We think that happiness can be caused, and so we design life plans which are supposed to bring us happiness. Even if we fulfill every aspect of our plan, we are disappointed. Everywhere we have sought happiness turns out to be a well of empty promises.

Happiness is really an effortless participation in life, without worry, without striving, without becoming. Happiness is freedom from the separate self, freedom from thought, freedom from attachment. True happiness is also freedom from seeking happiness. In wholeness of being, we don't need happiness as an antidote for boredom, depression, loneliness.

We do not want to admit that the problem of happiness has to do with the seeker of happiness. The seeker of happiness stands alone, separate from life, insecure and full of doubts.

Standing alone, separate from life, is what makes us seek happiness, which can never be found. The search for happiness ends when we recognize within ourselves that power which gave us radiance in the womb, which enlivens each cell of our body, which is behind every thought.

If you sincerely want happiness, and you have not yet found it, do not become despondent. You have a valuable opportunity. Try to find out who is pursuing happiness. This self-inquiry will show you that the seeker of happiness is in the way of happiness, and that when happiness is present, it is present without our knowing it. The Holy Grail of happiness is found only by those who completely and totally give up wanting and searching for happiness. In that profound moment, the wall of separation from life crumbles and the desire for happiness disappears. In that freedom, we are like flowers whose fragrance is "happiness."

Find out what happiness is, where it is, and how it comes about. Don't be a little bird, expecting your mother to feed you with predigested worms.

WHEN WERE WE BORN?

When were we born? If we were to face this question truthfully, without fear or ideas, our lives would be transformed. We would come to see the very source of our problems and conflicts and sorrows, and we would see how useless it is to try and solve the problems of our lives. Everything would be solved by finding out when — how — we were born.

It is very important to find out how we came to be. If we were to trace this notion of being, this concrete feeling of "I," we would find, first, thought, and then, emptiness. We came into being, not through our parents, but through thought, repeated over and over and over until that thought became an image in the mind. This image, this thought, exists within us, rooted in memory and time. This image is the fundamental thought which we project into the world. This image is what we send out, as on a Crusade, to reclaim the holy land of happiness. However, this image can never know happiness. This image of "I" that thinks of the future and plans and solves and achieves and experiences can never be happy.

We have endless conversations with each other about our lives, and we have simultaneous conversations, internally, with ourselves. The internal conversation is about perceiving and interpreting reality in terms of the "I," and its security, prosperity, and happiness. We are hardly aware of this internal conversation, but if we could hear it, we would hear that it is about us and about what we are afraid or hope will happen to us.

Shouldn't we first discover the truth of this "us," this "I" that is the sun in our personal universe around which orbit thousands and thousands of thoughts every day. We should see how we came into being. We would see that we are an image, of thought, and like thought itself, fragmented, anxious, and separate. When we become lost in thought, we live in fear. Our essential nature, which is a current of living awareness, is imprisoned in the thought of "I." This awareness, which comes to us in silence, in love, is really before thought, memory, and time. It is what the image of "I" tries to reclaim but always fails to do.

We have produced the problems we try to solve without success by becoming lost in thought. This image of ourself, seeking security, pleasure, love has instead found misery, war, hatred and sorrow. This will always happen, because we are in fact born out of fear, and it is this fear that has appeared in the world wanting freedom from itself by destroying its own face in others.

Sitting in silence, awareness can emerge from the shadows of "I." Awareness itself solves the problems. Awareness itself, the actual self, the real self, is what we seek. We are that which the image of "I" seeks in the future: we are not the image of "I," but the awareness behind it. When we see how we came into existence, we become love in that moment. We become free in that moment. We stop producing problems and conflicts and sorrows, in that moment.

WORK FROM THE SELF

We give so much of our lives to our work, so much of our time and energy and care. With this in mind, how carefully have we chosen our work? What exactly do we give ourselves to, and why? How many people are truly happy with their work? Have we turned away from a deep urge of the spirit, and settled for what is expected of us? Do we see work as strictly defined boxes, determined by others and our own self-concept?

Each of us has developed a set of ideas and beliefs about work. What are they, and how did we create them? What influenced our thinking, and are we trapped by that thinking about work and duty and responsibility? When we follow these thoughts, we will have conflict. Thoughts come and go by the thousands. How can we decide our lives based on thought? It is like building a house on quicksand.

Looking beneath thoughts, we find a different source for movement, action, and change. Each of us can find within ourselves an inspiration; literally a breath of spirit. This spirit will guide us if we listen, if we feel it.

A subtle, creative force directs this world. As the inevitable flow of life continues day after day, this creative force goes about its work, whether we are aware of it or not. This force is not something separate from life; it is life itself — intelligent and dynamic. It is within us, too, and it directs our individual lives, just as surely as it does the tides and the seasons and the orbits of planets. But we are often at odds with life, trying to swim with our thoughts and ideas upstream. When we feel frustrated and unhappy, we try to think our way out. Our conflict deepens.

Our effort to think our way through life produce the conflict and disappointment we attribute to circumstances. Is it possible to act correctly without effort, thought, and planning? Can you remember a time when you felt an inner current take hold of you and push you in one direction or another? This movement is, in effect, choiceless. We are compelled. We might say this is choiceless action, and this comes from our wholeness, from the creative force.

Any movement that reflects our unity with the creative force will be free of internal conflict. Acting from our wholeness restores us to life and frees us from doubt. The work you are meant to do will overwhelm you, you won't be able to prevent it.

Find out if you are suppressing the movement of your creative spirit by following ideas of what you should do.

Poonjaji, an Indian sage who lives in Lucknow, said, "When you start thinking and doing, then the trouble starts. This is a very stupid habit. Not thinking is excellent. Everything will happen. Something else will arise from you. A supreme power unknown to anybody will take charge of you and function through you."

Don't try to make your life turn out. If you move with your thoughts, there will be effort, motive, and desire. All of that comes from the mind. The mind will never be happy, never satisfied; that is its nature. All conflict is rooted in non-acceptance. Accept things as they are, totally and without the slightest judgment. Do not resist anything. In this environment, freedom and wholeness appear, and then whatever must happen will happen. We will know what to do and when to do it. When we have dissolved conflict in complete acceptance, we enter, fully and consciously, the dynamic flowing river of life.

Let it all go. Return to the source within yourself. Be the peace that you are. In that peace, in that inner stillness, the creative power will restore you to wholeness, and out of that wholeness will come the appropriate movement. You will not have to think about it. You won't be able to prevent it.

There is a wonderful saying that originates from a Native American tribe: "Sometimes I go about pitying myself, and all the time I am being carried on great winds across the sky."

FLY-FISHING
IN THE SIERRAS

A client of mine told me the real reason he goes fly-fishing in the Sierras. He didn't particularly care for fishing, but he said it was an acceptable excuse to stand all day thigh-deep in a mountain stream, surrounded by trees and rocks and clouds. And stillness. And the welcoming friendliness of nature. And the comforting current of the stream.

He would lose himself while standing in the streams of the Sierras. He said that the beauty and silence of nature drew out his soul and liberated him from the anxiety and pressures of his life.

He said that the top of his head would open, and something of him would fly up and out and finally hook in the mouth of a fish swimming in eternity.

And yet he could not directly face this, could not directly admit his yearning for this communion. He pretended to love fly-fishing. He didn't just come right out and say to people that he hiked into the mountains to feel his soul and connection to fish swimming in eternity.

Many of us are secretive about our longing to unite with the larger beauty of which we are a part. Why are we embarrassed to admit that we want to live in this pristine wilderness of spiritual communion?

I wondered at the impact this man would have if he had returned to work trailing the billowing clouds on a string, as open as the mountain skies, as honest as the trees, as articulate as the stream, as patient as a seedling awaiting the right time.

FABRICATING
OUR PROBLEMS

Each person I speak with claims to have a problem, issue, or confusion about some aspect of their life: work, relationships, self-expression, self-confidence, spiritual growth. These problems are like bullies who kick sand in our face and run us off the beach. We miss out on life; we can't enjoy the sea breeze and birds. Instead, we spend our time hiding at home, thinking of ways to avoid or beat the bullies.

To my eyes, no one actually has a problem, issue, or confusion. We pretend to have problems by creating them.

This small distinction is very important; it is not semantics. If we in fact have problems, we'll have to resort to all kinds of strategies to solve them. We may or may not be successful, depending on whether our strategic choice and effort is sufficient to the task. If, however, our problems are self-created, we have but to dissolve our own creations. In order to do this, we need to see the precise manner in which we imagine our problems into existence. This seeing is itself the solution.

There is a difference between our perception of "having a problem" and a situation which requires our attention and energy. A problem is a distortion of a situation. The distortion comes from our projected fears, insecurities, self-images, and limiting beliefs. Our experience of a problem is really the experience of these projected mental imaginings. The situation that calls for our attention and energy has become a horror movie. We can't see what needs to be done, because we can't see the situation clearly. We see only our own movie, and nothing we do within the movie will ever impact the situation, because they are fundamentally different.

Pulling the plug on the projector dissolves the movie about who we are and about what we think is happening. When we stop projecting our own mental activity, the situation at hand reveals itself simply and clearly. Our true Self is also revealed, simply and clearly, without imagination and projection.

What we discover about ourselves is that we are united with the supremely free, creative, and powerful force that manifested this entire universe! We discover that within our own Self is an unlimited capacity for knowledge, presence, and action.

Seeing the way in which we create problems and discovering the truth about who we are is the only strategy we will need to live with clarity, passion, and purpose.

BEING IS ENOUGH

Why do we want to change? Of course, we look around and see the chaos of the world we have created; we say this must change. We compare ourselves to people in the television or on billboards and we say that we want to become like them. Or we might want to lose weight, quit smoking, become more serene.

If we want to change, then we are resisting what is happening now. Why do we resist what is happening now? What is this resistance?

The resistance comes from a judgment and a rejection of our present experience. The basis for the judgment is our internal structure of self-image, beliefs, expectations, and desires. Isn't this why we want to change, to preserve that structure and to have our lives conform to it?

Are we seeing what is actually happening when we want to change something, or do we only see our own structure of judgment projected on to the situation?

Can we even experience what is actually happening now when we are in conflict with it, when we judge and reject and want to change it? If we can't even experience the present, how do we know it needs to be changed? Are we afraid that if we don't act from judgment and conflict that nothing will happen? We think we have to muscle up to life and shake the hell out of it.

We never actually change, though; we only change the means by which we think we will change. We can't properly change anything if we act from the tension and pressure of the mind. This is like a dog chasing its own tail. Wherever we look, we'll see the tail of our own mind, its projections, and our reactions. Krishnamurti said, "The crisis is in our consciousness, not in the world." First, we need to change our consciousness. It is the restlessness of the mind that keeps us on a treadmill of change.

In order to see what needs to change, stop trying to change. In silence, we can clearly see the congestion that leads to the symptoms which we want to change. We can see why we are in conflict and how that conflict is an expression of self-suppression. We will see how to dissolve that pattern to release the free flow of the natural energy of the Self. This is the real change we all want, the deep movement from self-suppression to freedom. This is not change; this is liberation. In this way, without changing, we are changed — restored to the harmony of the Self. To be in this state of repose with the Self is enough. Being is enough. This beingness is so perfect that even in rush hour at Grand Central Station, no one would bump into another. Everything happens at just the right time, in just the right way.

First, we should become liberated; then we can see what remains to be changed. What needs to change, will be changed by the power of liberation.

ADDICTIONS

Practically speaking, an addiction is something we can't do without, something we are enslaved by. An addiction is an habitual practice, the cessation of which causes severe trauma. Addictive behavior means to serve at all times and at all costs that to which we are addicted. We are not able to live without our addiction. Addiction is to be terminally dependent. One day, something within us awakens to the condition of our enslavement, and wants freedom. Wanting freedom, we seek out and enter an appropriate "recovery" process.

In this recovery process, we begin to discover the particular causal roots of addiction: how we want to medicate or escape tedium, self-loathing, existential isolation and loneliness. The object of our addictive behavior is like a rapturous distraction and avoidance of our present experience. Something in our present experience is compelling us to find solace, repeatedly and with great vehemence, elsewhere. We find something to get us elsewhere, and that becomes the object of our addiction.

What is it we can't face? The intensity of emotions? The depth of fear? The tremendous ache of loneliness or despair? The realization of impermanence? The intuition that we are not what we have been told we are, that we are not just a physical body and mind, but that we are the Self that shoots out like a geyser of light to unimaginable realms?

Are there many kinds of addiction, and are there many causes? We have heard about chemical dependency, and that our bodies develop a craving for certain substances, like nicotine or heroin. We have heard that, psychologically, we crave certain relationships and can't imagine ourselves independent of them. We will suffer all kinds of abuse, as long as we can remain in the familiar structure of that relationship. It is the familiarity that provides the support. In this familiarity is the known. and we are shielded from seeing exactly the condition we are trying to escape. In a sense, the consummation with the object of our addiction helps us avoid a confrontation with the insufficiency of our experience. It is not really the object of our addiction that is the problem; it is the quality of our experience about ourselves and our inability to face this that is the problem.

The object of our addiction becomes the solution to a problem of self. What is the problem of self that requires solution — whether the solution be medicated suppression or escapist transcendence? Don't answer immediately, don't rely on what you have read or heard to fashion a quick and ready answer. Take a few minutes to look directly at your own condition, and what you want to medicate or escape.

Addiction is not just wanting, it is craving. Why do we crave something, and what happens when we fulfill this craving? Having fulfilled our craving, is our craving over?

The question of addiction takes us right into the heart of freedom. Can we ever be free if we must have something? How does this condition come about in the first place? Why do we crave, why must we have something? Do we crave something to stabilize us, to comfort us, to provide security and relief because we feel we are spinning wildly out of control, without direction or purpose?

In the moment we awake from sleep, before anything has stirred, what do we crave? There is no craving. There is silence, peace. Before thought, there is peace. There is simple awareness, a breeze of pure awareness. This awareness attaches itself to thought. Thought itself is anxious and fragmented. Pulling away from the pure breeze of awareness, we become enslaved by the anxious undertone of all thought. This anxiety creates a sense of existential emptiness, and then we try to fill that impossible cavern.

We think of dependency in terms of substances or relationships. But let's look deeper. What happens when we can't watch our favorite television program? When the morning paper isn't delivered? How agitated do we become during a power failure, when the lights and computers and phones stop working? Think of everything that would cause you severe trauma to be without. Hot running water? We might think this is all harmless, but what would our condition be without the conveniences and conventions of our life? Would we be free from trauma? Is anyone free from addiction? Is anyone complete and whole, without fear and craving?

We love routine, habit, predictability. We don't view our normal expectations as addictions. If the test of addiction is the trauma of deprivation, can we face the enormity of our addictions? What about our very life? When we contemplate our death, do we do so serenely, with understanding and openness? If one is sincerely trying to live freely, creatively, we must wonder about all of this, and try to find out if we can live without the trauma of deprivation stalking us from the shadow of our craving. Is our dependency on entertainment any less harrowing than the dispirited figure lurking in the crack house?

Our whole life is an addiction. We are propped up in a hundred ways that we don't notice. We might think that these things are a natural part of living, that we are entitled to them, that they sustain life in a reasonable way. Is this true?

We are also addicted to our view of reality. We are addicted to our religious beliefs, without which we would be lost. Our identities and roles and beliefs are all addictions, aren't they? Can we give everything up and be free? Are we not addicted to having our own way, to imposing our will on events. Are we not addicted to our past? Please find out exactly what you can give up without trauma. Is there anything?

If we look at addiction in this larger view, not just our dependency on drugs and alcohol, who is not an addict? Is a politician not addicted to power? Is an evangelist not addicted to rhetoric? Is a scientist not addicted to proof? Is a business person not addicted to profit?

When are we not leaning on something?

It is a shock to see our own addictions. If everything we depend on were to be taken away, who would we be. Are we not ad-

live without this? Let's be honest, and look precisely at the whole issue of addiction, the whole process by which we depend on something to keep us intact.

What does this realization of our addictive nature tell us about ourselves and the patterns of our behavior?

An addict will do anything to preserve access to that which he is addicted to. Will we? How much hostility, violence, greed do we rationalize in the name of our unexamined addictions? What happens when someone threatens to deprive us of our addiction? The addict will do anything. Isn't so much of our compulsive, chaotic existence manufactured by our addictions?

Sitting silently, without movement in the mind, can we see the first impulse of craving? Does this urge come first, or does something else come first? Find out. It takes courage and honesty to see our whole predicament; otherwise, we will be enslaved without knowing it. We fight so hard for freedom from external oppression, should we not want to be equally free from internal oppression, from the slavery of compulsion and craving?

If we can see when craving is absent, we will understand addiction and what to do about it. Has one ever sat in a forest at night, unafraid, bathed in moonlight? Listening to the rustling leaves, the earth's breathing. Something opens within us, and this opening is empty and solid at the same time. Profound stillness of mind. A quivering in the heart of what is wordlessly present. In this depth of being, without movement, utterly still, is a total absence of craving. Returning to silence, to our source, reveals our wholeness, and we see that all addiction comes from a forgetfulness of this. Awakening to our Self is freedom. In this freedom, we are not terrified of the unknown, we embrace it. We are not partial; we are whole. We remain before thought, open and free.

If one wants to become free from an addiction, one must understand all addiction. To see what addiction is, we must see how much of our sense of self is determined by what we crave.

Have ever experienced a moment of true freedom? Have we ever experienced complete independence, from substance, from compulsive relating, from becoming? Are we not addicted to think-

Have ever experienced a moment of true freedom? Have we ever experienced complete independence, from substance, from compulsive relating, from becoming? Are we not addicted to thinking, to projecting our fears and anxieties into the future? What would happen if we gave this up? What is left if everything we use to define ourselves is taken away?

This can't be easily answered, because the answer becomes another support. Without holding, without pushing away, without anything, who are we? Is it possible to live in purity, without conditions and qualifications?

In a moment of awakening, of experiencing our innate wholeness, craving disappears. There is no other thing to depend on, no other place to go, no other time to covet. No condition to medicate or escape, no whole to fill. In this awakening to wholeness is simplicity, the joy of everyday life, the acceptance of everyday thoughts and feelings. No need to run, no need to hide, no need to fear, no need to crave. Simplicity is openness and wonder, simplicity is peace. Peace is who we are. When we know who we are, we are free, and this freedom dissolves the condition that is the root of all cravings, attachments, and dependent identifications.

FULFILLMENT

What is fulfillment? What exactly do we mean by this? It is an important question because so many of us stalk this quarry without ever finding it. Fulfillment is our snow leopard; we search and search and at the most we see an old footprint.

To become fulfilled means to be full. When we are full, there is no room for anything else; we are satiated.

If we were to slow down the process of our experience to examine everything frame by frame, what would we find? We find that fulfillment is not experienced through conditions or the attainment of the objects of our desire. We find, instead, that what we call fulfillment — fullness, wholeness — is realized at the instant we become quiet, when we release the fast forward button of our mind, when we stop chasing objects of desire, when we stop manipulating circumstances. You can see this for yourself, frame by frame, in slow motion.

We have been taught that fulfillment is to be attained through achievement or experience. Whatever can be achieved, whatever can be experienced is other than our own Self. Being separate, it exists in duality. It is the object, we are the subject.

Fullness does not exist in duality. If we could experience fulfillment in experiences and states and objects, we would not be interested in knowing our Self. We become dissatisfied with this approach, and dissatisfaction is good. It will put wood on the fire of inquiry. We can use this dissatisfaction as fuel to find out what and where fulfillment is.

We wander in this world of objects and desire, seeking fulfillment, but it never happens. It happens only in that moment when the desire and the object of desire merge into a unity. There is a glimpse of the fullness of non-duality. We are not aware of possessing the object, we are not aware of ourselves. There is an absence of self, of desire, of object. Is this not true?

Here is a paradox. In order to be full, we must be empty. If our emptiness is total, we become supremely fulfilled.

THE ROOT OF FEAR

There is a difference between the concept of fear and the actual fact of fear. We have to see what fear is in the precise moment it arises within us. We have to know our fear directly, not as a concept, not as a problem looking for a solution, but as it is before we react to it. This seeing of fear will liberate tremendous energy within us.

Have we ever tried to see fear at the instant of its conception, before we have named it? Will we know what fear is if we define it, explain it, and develop strategies for coping with it? Can we see it absolutely, as it is, without wanting to understand it?

Understanding is representational. It comes to us after the fact, as an abstraction, a thought, or an image. The thing itself is named and relegated to a fixed place in the library of our accumulated impressions. That which is most true and beautiful is without name, without representation — without even an observer, which is also a representation. If we are to truly know something we must erase its objectivity; we must erase our subjectivity. This doesn't seem possible, but it happens.

We have to leave ourselves behind and enter music in order to experience the truth of music. We must leave the listener behind. This doesn't sound rational; nonetheless, we know it is true.

Seeing, distinct from understanding, has this quality. Seeing is a direct comprehension of something before it has become represented in the mind by labels, associations, and structures. It is witnessing the instant of creation. This seeing of fear will illuminate and eliminate fear.

What are we afraid of? That our money will be stolen? That we'll get sick and die? That we'll have no one to love or be loved by?

That we don't look the way we're supposed to look? Are we afraid of what we've done in the past, or of our desires in this moment? Are we afraid that others will not respect and admire us, that we won't be liked? Is there ever an end to fear?

We usually try to remove, solve, or placate the object of our fear. Our syntax is I am afraid of... If we conquer what we are afraid of, whether it's public speaking or skydiving, does that put an end to fear, or have we just pushed it away with the strength of willpower and adrenalin, techniques and practice? Have we seen what fear is, and can this seeing eliminate fear from every cell in our body?

A few years ago, I was living in Austin. I remember one evening in particular. I was sitting on the steps of my front porch. The light was fading and shadows began playing through the trees, and what had been clearly visible in the light of the afternoon was now obscured. Suddenly, my whole body tensed and froze, my breath became shallow and rapid. I jumped up and back, my eyes fixing intently on a snake that had appeared on the brick walkway, just in front of my feet. In less than a second, automatically and without my conscious knowledge, all of the antipathy toward snakes that I had accumulated took possession of me.

When I had removed myself from harm's way, I relaxed a little bit. I looked again at the snake, and this time I saw a large twig that had fallen from a tree. The "snake" had vanished and so did my fear.

Does fear live in the objects we name? Or is fear a projection from within ourselves onto the world around us?

Where is the source of fear? Is it outside of us, in other people, in circumstances, in objects? Is fear provoked by what we imagine? Does fear have a legitimate life, or are we deceived because we have never examined what arises behind the word "fear"? Don't run from fear, don't stay in front of it, don't try to solve it. Turn within and face it, silently. If we can first see where the trembling begins, we can then look closely and see what it is.

Fear is the shadow of our own separate self trying to find a secure place in its world of false imaginings. Fear is the mind itself. The mind itself is always afraid, reactive, and self-protecting. Costumed in separateness, fear is our shadow. Feeling ourselves to be this body, this mind, the impressions of the past, we are vulnerable to everything beyond our control. In this vulnerability, our survival is always at stake. When our survival is threatened, fear steps forward. As fear steps forward, we can witness its creation. The birth of fear is in the womb of "me."

In the realization of our essence, fear disappears. Who we are is not bound by conditions. Conditions exist within us, as clouds exist within the sky, and are constantly changing. We are not affected by the roiling of events. We are not affected by the turbulence of thoughts and imaginings. When nothing that happens affects us, there is nothing to be afraid of. When we discover our essence, fear ends. Our essential nature is like the morning sun to the night of fear. This sun hovers at the highest point in the sacred hub of the heart.

ANGER

We have been told many things about anger and what to do about it, but do we know what it is, not by definition and explanation, but through seeing it as it comes into being? We can't deal effectively with anger, because anger is just a word. Anger is an advertising billboard, a broad concept that obscures the fact behind the concept.

What is it that we are referring to? Have you ever seen directly the forces that arise within you before you label them anger? Have you ever faced your anger as it materializes, or do you become immediately victimized by anger, certain of its reality because your conceptual thinking has legitimized it as something, like a rock or a flower or a chair?

We can see the ravages of anger in ourselves and by the effect it produces around us. But what is it?

Anger refers to a constellation of energetic responses to life, to our own thoughts, to our own actions, and to the thoughts and actions of others. What is the motive behind the energetic response? If we take away the word "anger" from our experience, if we do not react to that label, full of associations and recriminations, what are we left with?

We become angry when someone or something threatens us. We become angry when what we believe we are — our ideas and loyalties, our hopes and wishes — is threatened. We become angry when our security and well-being are threatened. But is this anger, or is it fear? When we are threatened, does fear arise first, and does that fear mobilize a self-protection response that we call anger? We can see that often our anger is really fear. If this is true, we must understand our own fear.

We become angry when we don't get what we want, when our will is thwarted. If this is true, then we must understand the nature of desire and will.

When we say anger, do we mean boredom or disappointment? Is anger really frustration? If this is true, then we must understand our own emotions.

Is anger really internal conflict between what is true for us and what is expected of us? When we suppress our inner truth, for whatever reason, we will eventually erupt, because we can't live forever in falsehood and self-betrayal. If this is true, then we must see the cause within ourselves of self-suppression.

Do we use anger as a means to control others who do not have the strength to stand up to us? If this is true, then we must understand our urge to dominate.

Do we use anger against others who try to coerce and manipulate us? If this is true, then we must see the roots of our own insufficiency and powerlessness.

Do we confuse anger with words and actions committed with a clarity and intensity that, while appropriate, violate some idea we have of ourselves? If this is true, then we must examine our own self-image.

We can't grapple with the phantom of anger until we first see what is moving within us before we label it, before we become victimized by our thoughts and feelings about the billboard called anger. This takes discipline and patience. We will have to encompass the arising energy with awareness in order to see it. As we encompass this arising energy with the spaciousness of our awareness, we can more effectively express what we need to express, we can act without conflict and bitterness. When we don't know for ourselves what is happening within us, the "anger" will control us. We won't know what to do even as we are torn apart. We'll continue to project this confused state onto others. We'll become more angry, then hostile, and then violent. If we are to end the ravages of anger, we must know what it is.

Will you take the time to investigate this on your own? Will you face these arising states with steady breathing and an open mind? Will you see behind the word, will you become intimate with the energy itself? Any technique or strategy for dealing effectively with anger will not free you from anger. Anger will survive and continue to torment you and others. Let yourself settle into silent observation of the tremors of extreme energy as it arises. Don't obscure what is happening by taking refuge in labels and concepts.

WHO IS THE NON-DOER?

Someone recently shared their concern about becoming apathetic in their practice of non-doing.

Why are we concerned with non-doing? Where did we learn that concept? We shouldn't even bother with it. All we can do is entertain a concept of doing or not-doing. Real non-doing can never involve the person who is concerned with it. Non-doing does not refer to anything we can achieve, nor is it some strategy for more effective living. Non-doing simply points to the fact that we cannot locate within us an entity that does everything we take credit for. For example, we know that we think thoughts. We can experience thoughts and their effect on us. But we cannot find the thinker of those thoughts. We can only say, "I am the thinker." But the "I" to which we refer is just a thought.

So it is with doing. One can say that there is action, and actions produce an effect. But the initiator of those actions is just the thought "I did that." We can't locate the "I." The more we concern ourself with non-doing, the more we will be caught in the web of doing. We will reinforce the thought "I did this" with the subtler thought "I did not do this," and we will deepen our confusion and separation from the Self.

When we see for ourself the truth of doing and non-doing, we won't have such troubles. It won't do us any good to understand this as a concept; we must see it suddenly and starkly, as a flash of lightening against the dark night.

One of Lao Tzu's poems comes to mind: "Do you imagine the universe is agitated? Go into the desert at night and look out at the stars. This practice should answer the question."

Looking out at the stars, do we imagine the universe is apathetic? The same power that holds the numberless stars in the vast heavens is within us. Our only problem is that we identify with the "I" in "I am not-doing" or "I am apathetic." Can we find the "I" in "I am apathetic"? We can't. Apathy arises as a state after we have identified with a thought or an image. All identification will be a suppression of the energy of the Self, and we will feel the diminishment of that. It is not our natural state, and therefore it does not feel natural.

Still, we don't want to resist apathy, or try to change it. We just want to see what it is and how it comes about. That is enough. Put your attention on the Self. Stop living in your thoughts. Live in your Self, which is beyond all concept and limitation.

When you live in the silence of the Self, you won't be able to resist the changes that must be made. You won't be able to resist the potential that will be realized through you. You won't be apathetic, because you will not be defined by ideas and images. When a great storm of energy and activity is appropriate, it will come through you. When quiet evenings of reflection are appropriate, why not enjoy the peace and pleasant breezes?

When the Self becomes awake within us, we will lose interest in much of what we have been told to be interested in. This is not apathy.

PAST IMPRESSIONS

It is important to see that we are not going anywhere, that we are not becoming anything, that we are not attaining anything. If we don't see this, we will never be who we are. We will be like ghosts drifting forever in the false promise of becoming. We can see that freedom, the Self, is our reality — we can see this in silence, as the real background comes forward and imbues the world of forms with its light and presence. Having seen this, why does it appear to fade? Isn't this really the question?

Have you seen that no one can bring this background forward? Have you noticed that the harder you try, the more remote it becomes? Certainly, it isn't enough to pretend that you live in the freedom of the Self if you don't. If in your heart you are caught up in various fears, suffer from anxiety or self-suppression, or feel the toxicity of desire and unfulfilled wants, you must be honest about this. It is important to be as honest about proclaiming the imminence of the Self as it is about what plagues our minds and corrodes our hearts.

If you had not glimpsed the Self, you would not know that the fear, anxiety, and pride you speak of were in any way obstacles to be overcome or dissolved. You would just accept them as the totality of the reality available to you. Instead, you know they are not. How do you know this?

You know it because when these states of mind appear, and you become lost in them, you feel a contraction of your Self. You know this contraction is not who you are. But you can't do anything to become your Self, because that effort is another obscuring veil. The effort can only come from the separate self.

What is happening is that you are beginning to see the intensity of our fascination with the mind and its projections. We are tightly bound up in this world of the mind; our very sense of being comes from this mind.

In fact, our fascination has kept us in bondage for a very long time; according to Poonjaji, 35 million years. Cutting the ropes of this bondage takes persistence, sincerity, and a willingness to experience the dissolution of these layers of mind forms with which we have become enthralled.

We have created numberless worlds within our own mind, and at the center of each world is our separate self — another mind form. Each of our individual selves that resides at the center of each world created in the mind has become defined, or identified, with the world it lives in. It has become that world, and any threat to the existence of that world, threatens the existence of the separate self. Each world might be a thought, a belief, an experience, a judgment, a decision, a memory — any impression that is kept alive becomes a world, with a separate self at its center.

These worlds are what obscures the Self, the background that we know we are. All of these worlds float in front of the Self, and eventually dissolve back into the Self. But we must come to know this, and this knowledge arises as the last of the worlds has been released by the last of the individual selves. This is our predicament.

When one recognizes how many worlds there are between us and the Self, it can be very upsetting. We find world upon world, impression upon impression. Each one is fortified by a separate self, which must die so the world can dissolve. The separate self does not want to die. So the worlds, the impressions, persist.

Think how much it stings to see one moment of the play of ego, of a separate self. I'm not talking about knowledge about the ego, but about seeing its intensity and depth and hostility. Thousands of impressions crowd each cell of each body, and thousands more fill the storehouse of memory that we carry from one life to another. At the center of each is a separate self which does not want to die. This is our predicament.

Someone once asked the Buddha how long it takes to become

enlightened. He replied, "Imagine a mountain made of pure granite that is six miles high, six miles long, and six miles deep. Once every hundred years a bird with a silk scarf in its beak flies over that mountain. As the bird flies over the mountain, the silk scarf brushes lightly over the granite surface. You will reach enlightenment in as long a time as it will take that bird to wear away the entire mountain."

Every time we fly over the mountain of our own delusion, we threaten a separate self and its impressions, its world. Some may die peacefully, others may resist and fight. Still, we must point out each false self and its false world, and in that way the background will be freer to emerge.

There can be extreme reactivity upon seeing how much we identify will false selves, states of mind, past experiences and impressions and their emotional shadows. Our false identities, our attachments and resistances and fears will try to kill the bird of our own enlightenment as it flies over us and touches us with the grace of the Self. We must see all of this, because it is the only thing that obscures the Self, the reality that we already are.

Still, the Buddha's story is just a story. Being who you are does not take any time, and no effort is necessary. The false worlds are just that: false. The impressions and memories and individual selves are created by the mind, and the mind is created by the Self. Even delusion exists already within the freedom of the Self.

FREE FALL
THROUGH TRUST

W hy are so many of us concerned with developing trust? Trust is a weight that we put in one basket of a scale to balance the weight of distrust we have put in the other. It is only meant to correct an imbalance, not create another one.

Life is always taking care of us, in that life is full and complete from one moment to the next. Our problem is that we have turned away from this into our own ambitions. These ambitions keep us away from life, keep us at odds with life, and it is for the sake of this inner conflict with life that we need a strategy to become secure.

Do you think that trust is a strategy for living that will never disappoint you, a guarantee for the security you crave? Will trust make things work out according to your wishes?

What is pushing us toward trust? Is it fear? Are we afraid that if we enter the stream of life — without distrusting, without trusting — we will experience hardships, deprivation, even annihilation? By trusting, are we trying to find a refuge from impermanence and the results of our past actions?

From a personal standpoint, we might want trust to insure that we are not hurt or criticized or ridiculed by others. This is reasonable enough. But aren't we just protecting that solid sense of self that obstructs the realization of who we are? We are not a solid self. Our history and story and apprehensions about rejection are not really true.

What do you see when you look around the edges of this impulse to trust?

What you will see is the fear of death. Not physical death, but the death of that within you which wants a life raft. We want to trust that we are doing the right thing, that we won't get hurt, that our dreams will come true, that others will approve of us. There is something we must see about ourselves that requires trust. What is it?

Behind this desire to trust is conflict, and behind the conflict, fear. Trusting will never eradicate fear; it will only cause the fear to go underground. Find out what you are afraid of, and dissolve that fear. When the fear dissolves, you won't need trust; neither will you distrust.

We can't see things are as they are through the lens of fear. When we see things as they are, we will not be afraid. Without fear, why do we have to trust? Without fear, we enter into life, without guile, and become buoyed by life in a fearless participation, moment to moment. If we need trust to live, we are still standing outside of life, bargaining and negotiating to have things go our way. Can we see what it is within us that craves this control?

In turning toward trust as a strategy for living, are we not defining ourselves by what will happen in the future? Do you see that our hope is that by trusting something, we will reap positive dividends in the future? By living in the future, we live in our mind. Living in our mind will never free us from fear and conflict. Trust will not solve the problem that we turn to trust to solve.

Without fear, without seeking security in the future, where is the need for trust? Life, of which we are a part, is an irretrievable stream of instants which flows constantly from fullness to fullness. Don't we really want to dive into this living stream of life, fearlessly and vividly participating fully in each full instant?

When the impulse to trust comes from a living depth within you, that is the beginning of the recognition of the futility of the separate self trying to control and guide the events and experiences in life, which are in fact governed by what you want to put your trust in. But seeing the fact of how life occurs dissolves that within you which needs to trust. By trusting the universe, or God, or the supreme power, it is meant that you should see that there is only that to begin with. You have invented a problem, and that problem must trust its creator to solve itself: this is absurd.

See clearly that within you which is afraid, which wants security, which believes trust is the way, and has imagined itself to be something other than a living expression of the supreme power. You only need to see the truth of who you are, and then trust becomes irrelevant.

INVITING THIEVES
INTO OUR HOME

We get angry at the people toward whom we should be grateful. We should be grateful to anyone who helps us see something about ourself that we had not seen before. This is how we become aware of our false imaginings and free from pettiness.

This is difficult, because we are quite attached to our false imaginings. They are our most treasured possessions. We think that whoever wants to take them from us is a thief. If a thief breaks into our home, we will be angry, not grateful. We'll call the police, and then try to stop or hurt the thief. We'll say damning things about them to others. If we bump into the thief even years later, we'll start screaming and shaking our fist.

We should be happy when a thief enters our home. We should immediately show them where our valuables are hidden and help them load our treasures into their car. And then we should offer them something to eat. We should treat them well, and be very grateful.

Most of us want to live in homes with expensive home security systems and guard dogs. We'll organize neighborhood watch groups and lobby for regular police patrols. We want an environment of extreme safety so our treasured possessions can't be stolen by thieves.

We can tell when a thief is about to steal one of our false imaginings, because we will feel a burning sensation, a fire that jumps from cell to cell. This burning is the alarm of our home security system. In this precise moment of our burning, with our house on fire, we should be grateful, not angry. Do not call the police or fire department. Offer the thief a meal. Once the burning subsides, you will experience the tremendous lightness and joy of freedom from pettiness and false imaginings.

It's true that this kind of burning hurts, but we get used to it. In fact, when we see what this burning does, we'll go out of our way to invite thieves into our home. When we see a thief, we'll smile and unlock the door.

Of course, all of life is a thief, if we have the courage to court the burning that frees us from pettiness. To see all of life as a thief requires an attitude of openness and gratitude for the opportunity to burn. It depends on what we want. We can, if we want, get all the way to the end of our life with each of our treasured delusions intact.

What do we want?

HUMILITY IS A GIFT

Humility is a gift of grace. We receive this gift when we experience the insufficiency of our own effort, understanding, and power to live in accord with reality.

Each of us has come upon a moment of crisis or despair in which we turn spontaneously to a higher power. We have come to the end of our rope; there is nothing else we can do. In this moment, when we turn away from our own effort and toward a higher power, humility is born.

Humility is the gift that comes to us when we have suffered enough at the hands of our pride and arrogance. But we cannot temper pride and arrogance by cultivating humility, because the humility we cultivate will come from our own effort. It becomes another strategy for empowering our willfulness. Humility is not a strategy for getting our way.

We cannot practice humility, we can only give ourself up in a sudden convulsion of recognition that the supreme power is in charge of this universe, not us. Then we receive the gift of humility, which does not define or belong to anyone. We do not become humble, we dissolve into humility.

Humility is the recognition that everything is sacred and exists in love. This love dissolves that which believes it is separate from love. This love is the underlying fact of all life, and it is the power that creates and sustains this world. When all contradictory thoughts have disappeared from the proud and arrogant separate self, then humility and love are born.

But we will first have to come to a thousand dead-ends of futility and frustration and sadness. We will have to first experience that our stubbornness against reality is a painful caricature. Then we will turn to the higher power. It is this power which is "humble," because this power operates in accord with reality, not with our individual desires, hopes, and wishes. Within the sacred hub of this power, we discover that everything is born of love, lives in love, and merges into love.

This recognition is humility.

NO SPECIAL OUTFIT

People often think that finding their purpose is like finding just the right outfit for a party. It isn't like that. One's purpose is not firm and unyielding; it is not a "thing."

We don't need any particular purpose. We only think we do because of an inner conflict with life. The origin of the inner conflict is alienation. In this alienation, we feel small, insecure, and ineffectual. We think that to find a purpose will give focus and meaning to this uninspired experience of ourself. It doesn't work, does it? We can't think or plan our way out of this inner conflict, whose roots are in alienation. We might think that if only we could find the right thing to do, we would be fine. Searching everywhere, we hope we'll come upon that outfit with our name emblazoned on the lapel.

Feeling that we must create or find purpose is a curse of our conditioning. We are conditioned to believe that, in order to live meaningful lives, we must become, achieve, produce.

Isn't this meaning but a justification for living? Do we need a justification for living? Doesn't this addiction to becoming tear us from our roots in life itself, which unfolds from moment to moment, each moment full and complete? When we are torn from our roots in life, we feel alienated, insecure. When we feel alienated and insecure, we search for a purpose to give us meaning.

Purpose and meaning are to be found in life itself, in living within the context of life's fullness and completeness, even as it flows and transforms, constantly creating new expressions of itself. If we think that we can find a static sense of purpose and meaning in this relentlessly creative flowing stream of life, we are going to suffer disappointment after disappointment.

To find our way back to an experience of our source requires absolute simplicity. Simplicity means to be like a snowfield of pure, uncorrupted whiteness. This simplicity is free from conflict, becoming, and anxiety. This simplicity is not moved by thoughts or pressures of past conditioning. It is pure, open, attentive, waiting without any expectation whatsoever.

In this pure waiting, the force of life will begin to move us in certain directions. Wherever we are moved, we meet that place with absolute simplicity, with openness, with appreciation. True purpose is to simply welcome with appreciation each spontaneous movement of the force of life.

Consider for yourself what is happening when you are not concerned with purpose, and consider what is happening when you are. Isn't is true that when you are not concerned with purpose, you are simple, open, and welcoming of what is?

Isn't it true that when you are concerned with purpose, you are alienated from what is happening, you are in inner conflict, you are looking into the future, even if that future is the next tick of your watch?

When you are free from the search for purpose, you are also free from your own individuality. You have become a part of the whole. You are not separate. You may be washing dishes, and feel purposeful. You may be leading a big company or starring in a hit movie. You may be watching a hummingbird. Does it matter what you are doing? Look at what is happening within you when you are not concerned with purpose.

You will find that you are not preoccupied with your separate self. Without this preoccupation, without this indulgence, you don't experience alienation, you don't experience inner conflict. You aren't concerned with purpose.

If you eradicate your sense of alienation from life, then each moment, each act will be redolent with meaning, because you will have become a part of each moment, each act. You will not be straining forward, obsessed with becoming. You will be carried by life, not by thought, not by ambition, not by greed, not by sadness, not by conditioning. We need only to be as simple as we are, in our essence. Let this essence move you, let this essence place you, let this essence flow through you. This essence will always appear in absolute simplicity. Your eyes will be open to true living, in all its beauty and subtlety.

If we allow the current that enlivens all living things to place us, to move us, we will be always exquisitely balanced and in accord with reality. This relationship to reality dissolves our alienation, and therefore our search for purpose. Being placed in life by the wisdom of the Self opens us to the recognition of the simplicity, purity, and perfection of each thing, each moment, each situation.

This is the true purpose: to find our way to an accord with reality, to see with our open and welcoming eyes this subtle beauty and perfection of life.

Please don't be satisfied with stuffing chocolates down the mouth of the separate self to suppress its alienation. You will carry a long shadow of sadness behind you and in that sadness you will suspect that the separate self's purpose is but a distraction, a temporary suppression of the experience of alienation, and you will still feel deep in your heart that you are weeping for the Self.

Don't try to find a purpose, just enter the stream of life.

OPENING REMARKS
IN CLASS

Usually when we think of being fortunate or coming into some luck, we think of winning the lottery. We don't generally think ourselves fortunate to have an interest in meditation, to have an interest in sitting quietly, to have an interest in turning the mind inward toward its source. We don't think ourselves fortunate because of this interest. But really, I think it's the greatest fortune that any of us could have, to come out on a night like tonight through traffic and rain and come sit quietly, peacefully, without any motive other than allowing the source of all things to manifest within us. We are very lucky if we are willing to release our customary self-centeredness and enter the furnace of silence, to be willing for an evening to not pursue anything, to not aspire to become something, to not harbor thoughts about oneself or others, good or bad, but to simply sit quietly and to allow the Self to appear.

This is the greatest fortune that a person can have, so I think we should appreciate our good fortune. My teacher used to caution against wasting one's life, saying, Before you die, find out what it's like to truly be awake; don't squander your whole life pursuing empty things.

To give oneself away in meditation, to forget oneself, to release everything that's known, to put yourself in a position so as to be taken over by something that the mind can't know, that's greater than the mind, is the fruit of good fortune. Then to take an active interest in it, to begin to do it regularly is even greater good fortune.

An interest in discovering the truth of who we are is not dependent on anything else. We don't use any of our talents. We can't come to it with any stature or status that we have. It doesn't matter what our net worth is. It doesn't matter what we look like, whether we have a husband or a wife, a boyfriend or a girlfriend, or a new car or an old car; it doesn't matter at all, any of those things.

There's something about an evening like tonight that will hold all of us spellbound, just looking at the rough beauty of a stormy night. There isn't one of us here who didn't at some point this evening take notice, didn't stop and look out the window or step outside, and look with wonder at this. Why do we do that? Why is this flicker of light so compelling? I think it's because it hits us very deeply. It reminds us of something. Just looking outward in a way that then makes us look inward to find the internal correspondence to that mystery and beauty and power.

This is also a form of self-forgetfulness. We just give ourselves over completely and in giving ourselves away there is always something left, there is always something that's there in the absence of ourselves. It's hard to give it a name. It's a feeling of pervading everything and being pervaded by everything. We probably wouldn't be off the mark if we called that love, maybe not the love that we refer to every day, but the kind of love that is a cleansing and settling, deepening, an opening to the Self with no thought that there is love. With that kind of love there is no wanting. You don't have to own anyone to have that love. You don't have to be afraid of losing anyone or anything to have that love. That love isn't a function of how much good work you've done or how successful you've become. That kind of love isn't a function of certain conditions; it's truly beyond all conditions. It just is. It's always there in silence. It's always there when our self-centeredness is spontaneously given up.

And then we look around and we don't know if there's anyone that we don't love. We can't find anyone we don't love. We don't even have to know them. We don't have to be known by them. We don't have to own anything or anybody. We can stand completely single, completely natural and be in that which we're calling love. And the pursuit of this love is behind everything that we do, and this love is the gift of meditation. So we can see how fortunate we are to have an interest in meditation, even if it's one time.

We might think we can meditate whenever we want to, that it

is our right to do so, like eating a big meal. But eating a big meal whenever we want is not a right. It is a rare privilege that most others in the world do not share. Look around; there are a lot of people who constantly struggle to feed themselves and their families, fighting with addictions of one sort or another, lost in a thousand anxieties. It is our good fortune to have an interest in the Self, to want to deepen our awareness and sit peacefully on the shore of inner silence. Please appreciate your good fortune. We have much to be thankful for. We have the time and the means and the interest to seek out the beauty and love that is within each of us. I do not know of a more beautiful way for people to be together. There is no competition here. No one is higher or wealthier than another. Whatever we may have accomplished or become, all of that remains outside.

What enters into this room is an urge to know ourselves, to see our innate wholeness, to fan the flame of our divine spark. This is why we come together, and it is this that we share with each other. What is revealed to us in these evenings, we take with us as we leave. For each night of class, there has also been a next day, the morning after, so to speak. We wake up with something of what is aroused here, not something remembered, but something experienced. It is something of who we already are that is aroused in this silence. We see something of who we are directly, because that's why we come together. We don't want to keep up our stories and dramas and dreams and fantasies. We want to see what we really are.

We all need love. This world needs love. It might not seem like much, when we look at the suffering in the world, to talk of love. But the love that is aroused here is what will alleviate the suffering of our families and friends, of our human family around the world. It is the absence of this love that drives us mad and makes us do terrible things. Let us continue for the next year to meet every week. Let us continue to arouse the love that is there within us. Let us try to share that with whomever enters our lives, no matter how briefly or for what purpose.

EMERGING WITHIN
THE REAL

Inquiry means to look immediately and directly at the fact of what is. This is the doorway to freedom. Freedom is never to be found in the idea of what is, projected onto the fact. Nor is it to be found in the memory of something heard or learned or even experienced. Memory is stale; it is old and already used up. Life, and therefore freedom, is in the fact of now.

Does that mean that everything we take to be a fact is real? No, but it is true; it is true in this moment because it is a fact for us. When we start with the fact of what is true in this moment, we can begin to examine it, to see it, to know it, and to discern whether it is real. We can begin to see that while something may be true for us in this moment, it is not necessarily real. And when we see for ourselves that something is not real, it ceases to be true. This is how we find out what we are, and what we are not. This is how we know what action to take, if any action need be taken.

This path of inquiry is about awareness. It is not about solving problems, or fulfilling our wishes, or changing the circumstances of our lives. Inquiry is a means of discerning what is real and what is not real. This seeing into what is real changes everything, without changing anything. We emerge within the real, and everything we are not falls away. When everything we are not falls away and becomes untrue, we and the world are instantly alive, fresh, new.

Inquiry and awareness feed each other. These are the first things. Don't escape into ideas and numbing dreams of what someone else has told you. Become aware of the actual process of your life. What is mechanical and habitual? What is conditioned? What is fear, insecurity, longing? What is spontaneous and free and real?

What is mind, and what is silence? What is fractured, and what is whole? Find out. Become aware. Don't be a slave to sadness. Find out who you are, see what life is. Question, examine, enter into silence. Become free.

WE ARE THE SKY

Silence is what we are. When we accept this, we become the sky. The sky is everywhere and nowhere, just as we are when we accept our own silence. Everything appears and disappears within us, within the sky; not the sky we see overhead, but the sky of the cosmos, the breath in which this universe appears. Clouds, planes, flocks of birds, spirals of dream, mountains, worlds upon worlds, space dust, and starlight — all appear in the sky without filling the sky. The sky contains everything.

The sky is always patient, never hurrying. Whatever appears within the sky one minute, will disappear the next. The sky is always just the sky, containing everything without effort or striving. The sky does not become what appears within it. Whatever appears, floats in the sky like sea froth on wave, visible but for a moment, than disappearing again, only to reappear on the next wave. To the sky, everything is like this froth, because the sky sees everything appear and yet disappear at the same time. Nothing stays longer than a moment, except the sky. No one knows how long the sky lasts, because it is not of time. It is not of anything. It is simply that in which everything appears and disappears. This is what we are. We are the sky.

Inner scientists and artists of the beautiful and musicians of silence and tenderness say that the sky, the silent sky, though eternally empty, has qualities. The qualities are experienced in absorption, by returning to the truth within us. The truth within us is silence, empty and full. It is empty, because everything that appears, disappears. The sky is always emptying itself. The sky has no hands to hold what appears within it. The sky has no desire, so it has no longing; it has no fear, so it has no anger. It is always emptying, as what appears within it disappears, and so the sky is always returning to fullness.

What are the qualities of silence? Can they be spoken? Can they be known? Or do we become them by returning, in silence, to the sky? After all, we are the sky. What would we be like if everything appeared and disappeared within us? Wouldn't we love everything? Wouldn't we be patient, forgiving, and playful? Wouldn't there be peace within our infinite heart, because there would be nothing to become other than what we already are?

In silence, we become the sky. This is where we find our fullness, our wholeness. To watch everything appear and disappear within us is very beautiful. It is easy to love, because we are so big! We have everything within us!

Looking in, is like looking up. We see the sky and relax. We relax so much, we usually fall asleep. But the falling asleep that happens when we become the silence is the waking up we dream of when we think we are who we aren't.

Look within. We are the sky. We are silence. See that. Be moved by that. Give yourself to that. Let the sky fill you up. Let the silence lead you. Give yourself to that. Peace.

CAN WE BE FREE?

Sometimes we are lifted to the tops of mountains or pierced in the heart by a shaft of love. A fragment of beauty may sting our eyes. Here is our freedom: in love, in beauty, in the silence of mountains gaining strength through patience, thousands of years at a time. Isn't this within us? Isn't the true person equal parts beauty and silence and freedom?

Are we free if we can do anything we want? Are we free if we can get anything we want? Or are we free when we have disappeared into life, and only life remains? What is between us and life? Between us and life are thoughts.

We may believe in ourselves, for example. We are very used to believing in ourselves. We can feel our own weight and complexity. Yet because of ourselves, we cannot see or feel life directly. We are like sentries trained to shoot life on sight. Our self weight has corroded our subtle senses. We can only experience life indirectly, through the thought of self. And then we have thoughts about thoughts. Of course we don't know this. We take it for granted. We even think that thoughts and thoughts about thoughts are what life is.

We are constantly at war with ourselves. We aspire to become something. Why? We work hard to prove something. We are constantly thinking and planning. Or we are going over in our minds what has already happened, or what we hope will happen. We want things; we don't even know why. We have preferences and fears. Deep pressures push us along. We are always straining. How did all of this come about? What is real? What is freedom?

Freedom is the disappearance, suddenly and completely, of the self which seeks to be free.

Where there is no self, there is no straining. There is no experience. There isn't anyone, just life. Life is all there is. Entering the oneness of life bestows freedom. In that oneness is silence. In silence is beauty, and in beauty is freedom. When our eyes see beauty everywhere, we will be in accord with reality. To know reality is to be free.

Freedom is to let go of everything, and then to drop the hands that have let go. Then drop the arms, the torso, the head. Drop everything.

"Do not be afraid of freedom from desire and fear," said Nisargadatta Maharaj. "It enables you to live a life so different from all you know, so much more interesting and intense, that, truly, by losing all, you gain all."

THE DRUNKENNESS
OF LOVE

Love is never absent from our lives. We do not have to find it. We are it. The problem is not that we don't know how to love, or whom to love in what way. The problem is that we are afraid of love, because love consumes us. We dissolve into love like salt dissolves in water. We disappear into love. We are overcome by love. Love does not disappoint us. We disappoint ourselves because we resist love; we are afraid of disappearing into love. And so we are confused about love. It eludes us. We can't quite grab hold of it.

We don't mind having the experience of love, but we don't want to lose ourselves. We only want to stand at the shore of love, dip our feet in, get a bit wet. But love wants more. Love wants us in all the way. Nothing short of drowning will be enough for love. To experience love, we have to lose ourselves. But if we disappear into love, our reasoning brain will protest. What will become of us, how will we manage? Don't get carried away, we could get hurt.

We don't find the love we are looking for because we are afraid of losing ourselves to love. We sit safely behind our emotional seawall where the ocean of love can't touch us, dreaming and imagining things, pretending that we feel love. This is fantasy love, thinking that love is an experience we have sometimes, under certain conditions. And the stress of trying to create the conditions we think will produce love is the very thing that defeats us, time and time again.

Love is not infatuation, excitement, or hopeful anticipation. Love is an inner ecstasy, an intoxication, a drunkenness. Love is the soft music that flows from life itself. Love is friendly to everyone. Love joins us together and connects us with everything. Love knows no fear or hurt. Love wants nothing because it is in itself full and complete. In this love there is no seeking love. In this love we know we are love. We feel this love flow from our veins to the farthest galaxies and back again. In silence, we know that we are love: our core is love. Love is within us.

We have to serve love, not use love, and stop trying to find love, to get love, to own love. When we realize that we are love, we become human. We go on living our lives, sipping from the cup of love, stumbling with drunkenness. Love is never absent from our lives.

WHY DO WE MEDITATE?

Why do we meditate? We meditate to show the mind the place from which it comes. We do this as often as we can. We do this every day, for weeks and months and years. We meditate until the mind relaxes and spontaneously releases its contents. When this happens, we become what we are, and no longer suffer from the pretense of whatever the mind might think we are. Whatever the mind thinks we are will always be false. The mind can never know who we are. The mind can never know the place from which it comes. It can only be shown, through meditation, that the place from which it comes is silence, and silence is not knowable by the mind.

The mind is the instrument of silence, of the source. But the mind, unable to know its own source, creates thoughts, feelings, images, concepts, and beliefs, and then projects all of this onto the screen of silence. That projection is what we think we are, what life is. The mind takes these images as being fundamentally real, and lives there. We live in these images because we identify with them; we become, through repetition, these images. Objects can be known by the mind. Silence, its source, is never an object of knowing, and can never be known by the mind. Silence is the knower of the mind.

The mind can only be turned toward its source until it spontaneously releases all of the images and projections of its own activity. In this moment, we become who we are, and the mind becomes what it is and functions at the appropriate time and in the appropriate way. Its projections of self are consumed in the silence, releasing its anxiety. We become what we are, infinitely present and aware, spontaneous and creative. We meditate to be what we are.

Meditation is dis-identifying with all of the thoughts and images created and projected by the mind. Meditation is the act of seeing that the images of the mind are just that, and that behind the mind is silence. Silence is awareness, and awareness knows the mind and sees its activity while remaining separate from it. This does not mean that we create an image in the mind of a watcher of other images. This does not mean that we lose ourselves in thoughts about the nature of the mind. Silence, awareness, is fundamentally different than mental activity. We can never know this, however, because silence is never an object of knowing. We can only become the silence, what we are, when the mind spontaneously releases its contents.

How does this happen? This happens as the inner awareness examines and sees directly the nature of thought and the impermanence of all mental activity. This is inquiry. Inquiry is a persistent examination of the nature of the mind. It is a means of seeing directly what ideas and images are, how they come into being, and where they go when they are not maintained through repetition and identification. Inquiry challenges the mind, inflamed and eager as it is to know, to formulate, to analyze. Inquiry finally traps the mind, does not allow the mind to escape into more ideas. When the mind is trapped, it spontaneously comes to rest quietly within silence.

Then we become what we are.

SEEING IS ACTION

There is a mysterious, creative force that directs this world. The sun rises each day, trees blossom in spring, days become shorter in winter. As the inevitable flow of life continues day after day, this creative force goes about its work, whether we are aware of it or not. This force is not something separate from life; it is life itself — intelligent, dynamic, pervasive. It is within us, too, and it directs our individual lives, just as surely as it does the tides and the seasons and the orbits of planets. Some of its work is welcome, conforming to our hopes and expectations; some of it is unwelcome, like weeds in the garden. We prefer that this force fulfill our desires, because we spend a lot of time and energy trying to make the events in our lives happen according to plan. When our plans don't materialize, we are not as happy, and often we try to bend life in the direction of our desires. We are often in conflict, at odds with life, trying to impose our will on life. The less our expectations are met, the more muscle we apply.

Does our effort to manage events pay off? Can we say that we always get what we plan for? Can we even say that when we get what we want, we are fulfilled and happy? Or does our very effort create the conflict and disappointment we attribute to "unwelcome" events? Is it possible to act correctly without effort, thought, and planning? Has this ever happened in your life? No choice about it, no conflict, just a spontaneous movement responding to the needs of the moment, the onset of winter. We might say this is choiceless action, action that always coincides with the creative force.

What does choiceless action look like? If you are standing near a tree and see that it is falling, you jump aside. Seeing and jumping happen instantaneously. We know exactly what to do and act decisively, without hesitation. There is no choice involved. If you stop to think about it, the tree will fall on you. The situation forces you to be present to what is. Seeing occurs in wholeness, when there is no separation between you, the falling tree, and jumping aside. Seeing is oneness with the situation. Actions arising from seeing are clean and precise, single, beautiful, graceful movements that reflect our unity with the creative force. These kinds of actions are always welcome, because they restore us to life.

When we act with life, we draw on infinite power and appropriateness.

This precision of action is also true when we see something psychologically. If we see that someone is abusing us emotionally, if we really see this, then that force of life will stand up within us and demand, "No, don't do that." If we get caught up in a series of reactive thoughts about the situation — "Who is she to do that to me?" or "I'll show her, I'll leave and then she'll be sorry," — our seeing will not be total, not complete. Unless we see the situation as it is, a clean, direct response cannot happen. Unless our seeing is total, our response will be inadequate. We will be left with a residue of conflict and doubt.

The secret to action is seeing, not thinking. It is choiceless, not willful. When our actions are an affirmation of our oneness with life, choiceless action occurs. The choiceless response to life is always perfect, always welcome.

TELL THE TRUTH

It is important to tell the truth. When we tell the truth, we stay on the straight road. We don't get lost in dead ends, fall into ditches, or have stupid collisions of inattention. When I say tell the truth, I don't mean that we are to act out everything that comes into our mind. Telling the truth is not an excuse to be obnoxious or unskillful in our relationships. I don't mean harming others or meddling in their lives. Telling the truth means to honor who we are at our core; it means we should not deny or betray our inner spark of life.

We think that by being true to our Self in each moment, something bad will happen. Actually, we are hurt only when we turn away from the pure impulse of the natural Self. We haven't seen this yet, because we are so used to shutting down and contracting in the face of disapproval, or anger, or threats. Or else we become reactive and hostile; we try to shut down the person who disapproves. Contracting within ourself and reacting with hostility to another are the same thing. In each case we betray the simplicity and integrity of the natural Self. So we learn to distrust our natural simplicity.

We think that it is the Self which gets us into hot water. It isn't. It's the contraction or the reaction. Walk down the path of being true to your Self a little more. See what happens. Nothing bad will happen. If something "bad" happens, see it as a natural re-direction of your life. If a door closes, another will open. If someone leaves your life, someone else will enter. We can continue to be friendly and open when we are true to our Self. It's quite startling. Kabir sang in one of his poems, "Just throw away all thoughts of imaginary things and stand firm in that which you are."

Being true to your Self also means accepting your life as it

I remember a talk that Muktananda gave in 197 when the world is seen through the lens of conventi we see men and women and a thousand other for But when the world is seen through the telescope o

turns out according to this inner faithfulness. We have to be willing to let go of the goals that have been created in moments of self-suppression. By accepting and following the expansion of the Self, one's life becomes very rich and satisfying, even if it also surprises us. Rumi wrote in one poem, "Find what expands within you, and water that." What a beautiful prescription for living.

If we live in this way, we won't know much more than the step we take now. We'll have to risk the anxiety of not knowing for sure. The future will become less vivid, but this moment will become very strong. We just follow expansion, and see where it takes us. We will see our goals only as they become manifest, one at a time, as we give ourselves to the deep creative movement that we normally avoid. We just have to go all the way. We can't give in to our own doubts, even when we become asthmatic from tension. If we follow what expands within us for as long as we have followed the tendency to deny who we really are at our core, we'll have another life altogether.

DYING IS FUN

The image of ourself, the "I"-thought, does not want to die. It wants to stay around and enjoy its own drama. If the "I-thought" smells its death, it lights up with fear. That fear, that anxiety, is the primary experience of the separate self. We think we are terrified of not existing. But when we don't exist there is no terror. This is not philosophy or speculation. We have all seen this, and we all know this. All of our "peak" experiences, such as the intensity of love, occur in our absence. In this resolution of duality, the disappearance of "me" and "other," there is a lucidity of experience, not belonging to anyone, that is more compelling than anything "we" could ever create on our own. We spend so much time trying to appease our apparent separation from life by collecting new experiences. Has anyone noticed that we do not exist at the end of the rainbow of ecstatic joy? We must die in order for rapture to be present. In this way, dying is good.

As the ideas and images and fears and memories of the separate self are washed out into the sea of pure awareness, a new person is born. That person has no name and no birthplace. There is a soft light shining in the eyes, an encompassing heart, a forgiving mind. The hands are open, not grasping, not pushing. Without doing, things are done. When help is needed, help is offered.

There is no point in preserving the very thing that obstructs the experience of the Self. We are happy to die, to drown in the ocean of infinite being, consciousness, and bliss. We only become afraid when we think about it. When we see that what we want requires the death of our smallness, the "I"-thought smells death and becomes afraid. It won't easily die. We have to make it into a game. Tell it that dying is fun, and that after it dies, it can go shopping.

THE REAL WORK

Sri Nisargadatta said, "Through the concepts of others, you have built up so many things around you that you have become lost to yourself. 'You' is decorated and embellished by the concepts of others. Prior to receiving any gossip from outside, has anyone any information about himself?"

Our real work is to obtain information about who we are, not through the gossip of others or the gossip of our own mind, but deeply. We must dive into the sacred hub repeatedly. We must learn to roam in that space and make love with its truth, until only that remains.

We shouldn't be content to live without finding out who we are. What do we really gain by climbing the highest mountains of achievement. Yaks and mountain goats can climb also. Should we just work blindly, carrying heavy loads from one place to another? Mules do that.

Within each of us is a spark of the divine power that created this entire cosmos. This is not whimsy. This is a fact.

Bhagawan Nityananda said, "The essential knowledge must be attained by everyone. What is this essential knowledge? For the individual self to know the mystery of the universal Self." To know the mystery of the universal Self is within our reach. If we don't reach for this knowledge, whatever we experience, whatever we do, whatever we achieve will all be in a dream from which we must eventually awake.

SURRENDER

A friend of mine, the pastor of a Presbyterian church, told me that a lot of people say that they want to go to heaven. Except, he noticed wryly, no one wanted to die.

It's the same with surrender. No one wants to give anything away. We love our individuality, our independence, our willfulness. And so we love the very source of our pain and ignorance. Isn't this odd?

Surrender means to give up false ideas for the sake of the true. It does not imply deprivation, but rather devotion. Devotion means to love what is true.

Each time we let a false idea go, we experience a tiny death. This is the real instant of surrender; the moment that the ego dreads is in this moment of the death of wrong understanding. Sufi Sam said that we don't like solutions which interfere with our concepts. We are so closely related to our beliefs that when they are about to die, we feel as though we are about to die. We want to go to heaven, but we don't want to die. We want to feed our delusions with vitamins and minerals and all kinds of supplements for eternal life.

One belief that we have a hard time letting go of is that the world is a material place. It is a physical world, but it is so in relation to our sense organs and mind. With a keen eye, however, we can see that this "physical" world is an undulating ocean of consciousness, of light masquerading as matter.

I remember a talk that Muktananda gave in 1979. He said that when the world is seen through the lens of conventional thinking, we see men and women and a thousand other forms and objects. But when the world is seen through the telescope of the Self, there is only scintillating consciousness.

These telescopes are given out at the door to heaven, and heaven is right here where we all live, if we will let die what must die in order to know this.

FROM THE PAN TO THE FIRE

How much time do you spend each day struggling to make your life turn out? Everyone I know spends hours and hours in one struggle or another.

As we struggle with our inner and outer life, we think the way to end the struggle is through some act of will. We will ourselves out of the frying pan of struggle with choice, decision, intent, desire, ambition, strategy.

Unfortunately, we end up in the fire of more struggle, more conflict.

The problem with willing ourselves out of conflict with life is that our will is the tension of the separate self. Using will to resolve conflict is like trying to pull yourself up with your own shoe strings. What happens? More will, more conflict, more tension. Nothing is resolved.

Our will is rooted in tension. Our tension grows from fear. Our fear is about our own extinction. We are afraid we won't survive, that our life won't turn out. In order to survive, we struggle. The struggle itself is conflict. The conflict is the separate self, at odds with everything around it.

Will is blind. We can't live happily and effectively using our own will to end our struggles and conflicts. What can we do?

We can relax. Does this sound too simple? It isn't. When we relax, we dissolve our tension, and then our eyes and heart open. With open eyes and heart, we can see and feel the subtle current of life wanting to nourish us and guide us. Rumi said, "Feel what expands within you and follow that." In order to feel this subtle movement of expansion, we must relax our tensions.

Look at your own life. There are times when you relax into an inner expansion of clarity. What follows is elegant and graceful, seemingly effortless. Our tension decreases. We just follow that expansion. This way of resolving struggle and conflict unites us with the harmony and order of the Self.

DOING THE RIGHT THING

W e don't need a conscience or code of ethics to guide our behavior. We just need to understand that we each have a backyard.

Our every word and action is a seed planted in fertile soil. Sooner or later, each seed will sprout, and it sprouts in our own backyard.

The Buddha was supposed to have said, "See yourself in others, then whom can you harm?" This is all the conscience we need.

We can't cut any corners on this one. We can't look the other way. We can explain and justify our behavior to ourselves and each other; nonetheless, the seeds are planted. When the time is right, they will shoot up through the dirt. Our rationalizations won't keep them down.

You can't blame anyone else for what appears in your own backyard. You have to look honestly at the seeds you've been planting.

Hardly anyone does this. We are so surprised when we look out the window and see ten foot weeds marching toward our back door.

Don't be surprised.

WE ARE ALL MOVIE STARS

There is a huge irony in life. It's so huge, we can't articulate it. We can only see it and laugh, and then go on living.

I see it every time I go to the movies. The characters think that the play is moved forward by their effort. They think that what they do and say in each scene will affect the next scene. Of course, the characters do not know that the whole movie is already written, all the experiences and outcomes already decided. They don't know that their every thought and action is scripted, their every word already encoded on the celluloid that has yet to unwind.

When we see a movie for the second time, we can appreciate this irony.

Until we know the Self, we are merely characters in our own movie. Thinking that our choices and decisions give impetus to the next scene, we energize our own drama. We can become very demanding and greedy. Our plotting can become dark and complex.

The drama in which we are all stars, like the movies in the theater, is viewed on a screen, a background, without which there wouldn't be a movie.

In theaters, the movie is projected against the background of a big white screen. It is created with the light of the projecter and the images of the film. In life, our drama is projected on the screen of the Self. It is created with the mind of the separate self.

We can't recognize the Self as long as our movie is playing, just as we can't see the white screen in the theater as long as that movie is playing.

What does this have to do with our life? Here is the irony. We have to play our part. We can't hold anything back. We have to roll up our sleeves, jump in, and give the best damn performance we can. But the play is already scripted.

Something in us knows this. From beyond time and knowing, we see this and laugh, and then go on living. But the living becomes different. Our living is no longer tense with an excessive concern for ourself. We don't give more force to the drama, propelling it forward.

Without tension, the mind becomes quiet. When the mind becomes quiet, the Self appears. When the Self appears, we notice that our part is suddenly more light-hearted, generous, and friendly. We sort of lean back and touch the screen.

We become the screen of the Self.

SONG OF FREEDOM

If we are seeking the real, the real is also seeking us. If we want to know the truth, the truth wants to know us. If we want to experience love, love is rushing toward us as light from a thousand inner suns.

Be like a child in front of this love, rushing toward us: don't move. Stand still. Don't try to find the real, or know the truth, or experience love. All effort pushes it away. Be like a lost child and wait to be found. Stand still, be open, look — now — and see what you want already possessing you.

We don't need to seek: we have already found. We don't need to learn: we already know. We don't have to become: we already are. See this and be free.

The world is alive and breathing inside your very body. All that you treasure is within you. Your inadequacy is but a habit, your bondage an illusion, your fears but shadows and gossip. Let go of all you cling to. Only you can free yourself from your own deception. Forgive yourself, step into the light of love rushing toward you from a million inner suns.

No one has harmed you, no one has wronged you. Only your pride thinks this is so. Let it go.

Bitterness is your own dark night. Let it go. There is nothing worth protecting.

Let the breath of new life fill you and fill your mind, and fill your body. Your cells are now vibrating with new life. Your heart is opening, your being is growing larger and larger, colliding with the onrushing love. In this collision you can dissolve without fear.

What you want is at hand. You cannot know it. Stop trying.

You cannot possess it. Stop trying. You cannot use it. Stop trying. Just give yourself to it without a thought. Go into the onrushing love fully. Resolve to end your suffering now.

You are that from which this earth has come. You are that from which the spinning worlds and vast heavens have come. You are that which came before and is now and will be. You can hold mountains in your hands, and hear the ants walk under leaves a continent away. You can heal disease, and sing the songs of stars and dolphins alike. You can reach without limit and you can awaken spirit everywhere it is sleeping. You are the infinite well of love.

Feel all of this. Open your heart to this. Join with that, for it is your real self. It is your true self. It is where love is.

Come out of hiding, come into the light, come into the world that is free of guilt, free of sin, free of fear. You can hold heaven and earth together. There is no separation, nothing to be separate from.

We know this, we have seen this. Let us live this, as it is, now and forever.

Begin to serve what you seek and what you seek will fill your cup to overflowing with love and holiness.

Do not believe you are helpless or unworthy. You can allow the divine power to claim you. Whose permission do you need? That is who you are. How long will you be imprisoned in the past? We cannot become whole: we were never broken. We cannot heal ourselves, we were never wounded. We cannot become pure, we are already pure. We do not need reasons to dance freely in the light of the onrushing love.

Give up the addiction to what is not true. How did this come about? Why do you insist on a lie? Why? We are not the helpless victims of sorrow or confusion or anger or humiliation. Throw these tiny pebbles back into the ocean of your Self, and be free.

What is holding you back, but your own attitude? This attitude is false, let it go. Awake, now, from your dream of imperfection. Throw pain and guilt into the ocean of your Self. Be free. Who has told you to be quiet and meek and oppressed by stupid conventions and false attitudes? Shake the tree of your real life hard, shake it wildly and bring down the golden fruits of your own divinity. Eat these, and give these to everyone.

We have brought terror into the world, but the world is not terrible. We have created enemies, but we are not. We worship fear, when it is love we want. We become sick, but we are luminous beings. We pretend to be petty and insecure, when we are vast and abundant. Please, let us awaken from our dream of imperfection.

We are already what we seek. We don't need to learn to love, we are love. Share this, give this, be free now — for love is eternal and you are that.

ABOUT THE AUTHOR

Robert Rabbin, founder of the Hamsa Institute, has had a life-long interest in the nature of the human mind and consciousness. In 1969, he began to practice meditation and research various spiritual paths. In the early 1970s, he continued his research while living in Europe and the Middle East. In 1973, Rob trekked over-land to India where he met meditation master Swami Muktananda, with whom he studied for the next ten years.

Rob now holds dialogues and leads retreats around the country and meets with individuals for private consultations. As an executive coach, Rob works with leaders from a broad range of companies and organizations, and has designed and led retreats for individuals and groups of over 300.

He is a co-author of *Leadership in a New Era,* and his articles have been published internationally in numerous magazines and journals. Rob is a frequent speaker to groups in the business, academic, and spiritual communities; and he has been interviewed in newspapers and on radio.

THE HAMSA INSTITUTE

- Private Consultations
- Executive Coaching
- Dialogues
- Retreats

If you would like to:

☐ be on Hamsa's mailing list,
☐ receive Hamsa's information packet,
☐ sponsor a program in your area, or
☐ personally discuss Hamsa's services

Please call, write, or fax for details:

Hamsa Institute
20 Sunnyside Avenue
Suite 118–A
Mill Valley, CA 94941
Phone: 415 389-0214
Fax: 415 389-0231

ADDITIONAL BOOKS

Additional copies of *The Sacred Hub* may be ordered directly from the Hamsa Institute.

Price List:
Copies
1 – 9 . . . . $12.00 each
10 or more. . . . . $9.00 each
(less 25%)

Note:
Resellers, distributors and libraries: please call the Hamsa Institute at (415) 389-0214 for volume discount information.

Sales Tax:
Please add 7.25% for books shipped to California.

Shipping and Handling:
Please add $2.00 for the first book, and 75 cents for each additional book. Books are mailed first class.

ORDER FORM

Name: _____

Address: _____

City: _____   State: _____

Zip: _____

Telephone: _____

Quantity: _____

Unit Price: $_____

Total Price: $_____

Sales Tax: $_____

Shipping: $_____

Total Enclosed: $_____

Mail order form and check or money order to:

Hamsa Institute, 20 Sunnyside Avenue, Suite 118–A,
Mill Valley, CA 94941